From Russia with a Toast:

a family cookbook

with toasts, traditions and superstitions

From Russia with a Toast:

a family cookbook

with toasts, traditions and superstitions

by Luda Kopeikina

Illustrated by Tatiana Voskresenskaya

Equanex Publishing
Boca Raton, Florida

ISBN 978-0-578-04955-7

Equanex Publishing Company
600 South Ocean Blvd, Suite 306
Boca Raton, FL 33432

First printing April 2010

This book is available at quantity discounts for bulk purchases.
Please e-mail to info@equanex.com
Visit our website: www.FromRussiaWithToast.com

To Kathy with deep gratitude for your magnificent presence in my life!

Acknowledgments

Compiling a book of family recipes is not a trivial undertaking and requires the whole extended family to contribute. I am extremely fortunate and grateful that my family took this project to heart. My sister, Tanya and my niece, Olga, were generous in taking time to write down their favorite concoctions and send them to me. Many of the recipes in this book were written by them.

Russians love to find occasions to sit around a table laden with good food and celebrate life by raising toasts, sharing jokes and discussing events of the day. Toasts are an integral part of the culture. This book contains just a sample. But even this sample would not have been possible to compile without the support and help of my dear friends, Sasha and Valya Livshin. Sasha knows many of these toasts and jokes by heart and we raised many glasses to the successful completion of this book while sitting around their dinner table.

As always, my first editor of choice is my wonderful daughter, Kathy, who did an outstanding job correcting this manuscript. My sincere thanks go to Tatiana Voskresenskaya who embraced this project as her own, producing great illustrations in the Russian style.

And finally, I could not have completed this book without the loving encouragement of my dearest husband, Igor, who always referred to this project as a 'monumental undertaking' which challenged me to get it done. I am sincerely grateful!

Table of Contents

Toasts

Traditions

Superstitions

Introduction

Every family has a set of favorite dishes that the whole family loves. When you think about these dishes, you remember the great taste but you also remember the warmth, the laughter and the joy of the family gatherings associated with them. And this is exactly the inspiration behind this book – to collect the recipes that record the great taste of our favorite dishes but also capture the spirit of joy associated with them.

In our family's case, the spirit of joy is also associated with toasts. This is why this book includes a sampling of toasts to capture this spirit. When we toast, we always say something positive about life or about the person that the toast is intended for. As a result, toasts fortify the wellbeing of the participants and inspire joy.

Toasts are also a Russian tradition. My husband and I were both born in Russia and came to the US in the early 80s. Russians love to sit around a table laden with food - eating, drinking and talking about what's happening in their lives, in society and in the world. They find any excuse to do so. One of the major parts of these gatherings is drinking and toasts. The beverages do not have to be alcoholic, we often toast with cups of tea. But we always toast.

People unfamiliar with the Russian culture believe that Russians are grim and gruff because this is what they often encounter on the streets and see being portrayed in the movies. But the truth be known, Russians are warm people when you get to know them, they love to laugh and they are masters at laughing at themselves. As a result, many toasts are jokes or caricatures with a message. This form of toast has been raised to a unique art form in

Russia, which, I believe, does not exist anywhere else. This book includes a number of these toasts that provide a small window into this culture.

Most recipes in this book have their roots in Russian tradition. Some of the classic Russian recipes got changed slightly with speed of preparation in mind. You will also find a number of recipes that were added to our family's menus over the last twenty seven years of living in America. Even though we all live extremely busy lives, we love to be able to quickly create a really delicious meal. Our family is no exception. Over the years we tried out a huge number of recipes and selected the precious few that are this way - delightful and quick to prepare from scratch.

Many Russian dishes came from Europe during and after the rule of Peter the Great in the 18th century. As a result, some of them will feel familiar. However, as you try them out you'll find that they are similar but different, with a new twist. If you like trying new things but want predictability in your results, this book is for you. Enjoy!

Luda Kopeikina
Boca Raton, Florida
February 2010

Russian Cuisine

Russia is a huge country spanning over 6,000 miles (10,000 km) from west to east across 12 time zones and several climate zones. It comprises more than 125 ethnic communities with their tastes and traditions. Over the course of history, the Silk Road, the Tea Route and the Trans-Siberian Railway connected distant regions and allowed them to influence each other in many ways, including cuisines. As a result, Russian cuisine is a fascinating multifaceted blend of regional and national tastes.

There is one characteristic, however, that unites all cuisines across Russia and it's how the food is served – with tremendous hospitality and in a pleasure loving way, full of cheer and joy.

In Russia, food is love.

Quick Bites

This section contains quick and easy appetizer recipes to keep guests happy while others arrive. The traditional Russian meal, however, starts with the course 'zakuski' that are presented in the next section.

Quick Bites

Avocado Dip

½ cup fresh cilantro
½ cup fresh parsley
¼ cup chopped onion
⅓ red bell pepperF
1 tsp lemon juice
1 Tbsp jalapeno pepper
1 medium size tomato
1 avocado
Salt and pepper to taste

Pulse the first six ingredients in a food processor until the desired salsa type consistency is reached. Cut tomato into slices and add to the processor. Core avocado and scoop into the processor. Pulse the mixture until chopped through. Add salt and pepper to taste.

Makes 1 ½ cups

Our family calls this appetizer 'vitamins and minerals on a platter'. It becomes more so since we serve this dish with sliced veggies rather than chips. It is delicious, easy to make and extremely healthy.

Spinach Dip

5 oz (1 bag) baby spinach leaves
2 oz cream cheese, cubed
1 cup shredded cheese
4 artichoke hearts, chopped
1 Tbsp mayonnaise

Buy artichokes that were preserved without vinegar if possible. Put spinach into a microwaveable dish and microwave for 1 minute or until just wilted. Squeeze slightly to remove the released juices. Add the remaining ingredients, mix and microwave for another minute or so. Mix well and serve with chips or veggies.

Makes 4 servings

This is a hearty appetizer for winter months. It should be served warm but can be made quickly just as guests are arriving.

A toast
If You'd Like To Be Happy

In the Caucasus region of Georgia, they say: "If you'd like to be happy for one day – get drunk. If you'd like to be happy for one week – pretend to be sick. If you'd like to be happy for one month – get married. If you'd like to be happy for one year – get a mistress. And if you'd like to be happy all your life – be healthy!" Let's drink to the happiness of all the people here – to your health!

Hummus

1 16 oz can chick peas
2 Tbsp tahini
2 cloves garlic, chopped
1 Tbsp lemon juice or juice of ½ a lemon
½ tsp salt
2 tsp any vinegar

Drain half the liquid from the can of chick peas. Transfer into the food processor with the remaining liquid. Puree chick peas briefly, then add the remaining ingredients and blend to a thick paste consistency. Taste and correct the seasoning.

Makes 1 ½ cups

We serve hummus thinly spread out on a dinner plate with regular olive oil drizzled on top. Lately we have been using spicy garlic oil. Yum!

Variations

This recipe can be varied easily with a number of great additions to create several distinct dishes:

- Add ½ canned roasted bell pepper or ½ bell pepper quickly cooked in the microwave.
- Add 3 sun-dried tomatoes.
- Add an avocado.

Baba Gnoush

1 medium size eggplant, about 1 lb
2 Tbsp tahini
2 cloves garlic, chopped
1 Tbsp lemon juice
½ tsp salt
2 tsp any vinegar

Roast the eggplant on a grill until blackened. Alternatively, prickle the skin of the eggplant with a fork and cook in the microwave until soft. When cool enough to handle, remove the skin by cutting the eggplant in half and scooping the flesh into the food processor. Add other ingredients and blend well. If the mixture is too thick, add drops of water or vinegar. Garnish with oil and chopped fresh parsley if desired.

Makes 1 ½ cups

Most people believe that eggplant is a starch. It is not! It's mostly fiber. You can eat as much as you want with no impact on your weight!

A toast
To Dreams

Life is short and our life span is limited, but our dreams are limitless. When you are going home, you are already home in your dreams. When you are walking to your lover, in your dreams you are in her arms. You live now, but in your dreams you are years ahead. Dreams go past the time when life ends… So, let's drink to dreams that prolong our lives!

Green Goddess Dip

1 ripe avocado
¼ cup sweet onions
2 Tbsp mayonnaise
1 Tbsp sour cream
1 tsp lemon juice (can be omitted)
Salt and white pepper to taste

Combine all ingredients in a food processor and process until smooth.

Makes 1 cup

This dip is extremely easy to make but is a wonderful crowd pleaser. We usually serve it with veggies.

A toast
Important Lessons

One merchant gave his son a coin saying: "You should start saving money, son." The son threw the money into the river. The merchant did not say anything. His son continued to live at home doing nothing. One day, the merchant asked his son to start earning his living. His son found a job. The job was tough but he made a little bit of money. When he brought the money home, his father said: "Go and throw it into the river." It was only then that the son realized how ungrateful he was. So, let's drink to our fathers and grandfathers who used wisdom rather than punishment to teach us important lessons.

Pesto Goat Cheese Spread

4 oz soft mild goat cheese
2 oz cream cheese
1 Tbsp sour cream
¼ cup pesto

PESTO:
3 large garlic cloves
½ cup pine nuts
2 oz Parmesan cheese, coarsely grated
½ tsp black pepper
3 cups loosely packed fresh basil
⅔ cup extra-virgin olive oil

For Pesto - with the food processor running, drop in garlic and finely chop. Stop motor and add nuts, cheese and basil, then process until finely chopped. With motor running, add oil, blending until incorporated. Add more oil if desired.

For Dip – Allow cream cheese to soften at room temperature. Stir together cream cheese, sour cream and pesto until smooth. Add salt and pepper to taste. Serve with veggies.

Makes approximately 1 cup

Pesto can be prepared and stored in the refrigerator for several weeks. As a result, this dip can be made quickly and easily when unexpected guests arrive.

Baked Artichoke
with Basil & Garlic Dip

1 large artichoke
½ cup basil, packed
1 clove garlic
3 Tbsp mayonnaise
2 Tbsp sour cream

Cut the top off the artichoke and then cut it in half vertically. Make an incision under the choke and then pull out the spiky leaves together with the choke. Rinse, put face down into a microwave dish with a cover. Microwave until the heart of the artichoke is soft, 3-5 minutes.

For the basil & garlic dip, combine the rest of the ingredients in the food processor and process until smooth.

Makes ½ cup

All French recipes call for the artichokes to be boiled or baked in the oven for 40-45 minutes. Such preparation requires advanced planning. As a result we rarely made this tasty appetizer. Microwaves to the rescue! Now we can enjoy the artichokes whenever they are available.

Variations

Try cilantro instead of basil.

Shrimp
with Basil & Garlic Dip

1 lb large or extra large shrimp

Devein, peel and boil the shrimp. Serve with the Basil & Garlic Dip described in the preceding recipe.

Makes 4 servings

This dish is using the same dip as for the artichokes. It is delightful not only with shrimp but with other types of seafood.

A toast
To Being Right

After a heated argument two people decided to ask a wise man for advice on their argument. The wise man listened attentively to one of them and said: "Yes, you are right!" The other then presented his point of view. The wise man also listened to him with full attention. And then said: "You are absolutely right!" The wife of the wise man interfered, asking her husband: "How can it be that both of them are right?" The wise man sat in profound thought for a couple of minutes and then told her: "You know, you are also right!" This toast is to those who are always right!

Guacamole

1 cup green peas
1 ripe avocado
½ cup fresh cilantro, chopped
¼ cup fresh parsley, chopped
1 tsp jalapeno peppers
¼ cup green onions, chopped
½ tsp cumin
1 Tbsp lime juice
Salt and white pepper to taste

Process green peas in the food processor, add all other ingredients except for the avocado and process briefly. Mix with cubed avocado and serve.

Makes 1 cup

The addition of the peas and the cumin make this dish. If you do not care for the cumin, you can omit it to get a more standard guacamole.

A superstition
A Barrier to Wealth

In Russia, it is believed that you will have no money if you use your bare hands to wipe crumbs off the table.

live Dip

1 16 oz can large pitted olives
¼ of a small sweet onion
4 oz cream cheese, softened
1 clove garlic, chopped

Combine all ingredients in a food processor and process until smooth. Serve with crackers and veggie slices.

Makes 1 cup

This dip can be made in less than 5 minutes. If you keep the ingredients as staples in the fridge and the pantry, this dip can be a wonderful guest pleaser.

A toast
Life is a Test

A wise poster says: "Life is a test. It is only a test. Had this been a real life you would have been instructed where to go and what to do." This poster is a great reminder that when we see each problem as a serious battle for survival, the only time we are likely to be happy is when everything is going just right. And we all know how often this happens. But, when we look at life and its many challenges as a test, or a series of tests, we begin to see each issue as an opportunity to learn and grow and a chance to roll with the punches. Let's drink to not taking life so seriously!

Salsa

½ cup fresh cilantro, chopped
½ cup fresh parsley, chopped
½ medium size sweet bell pepper cut in large pieces
¼ cup onion, chopped
1 tsp lemon juice
1 Tbsp jalapeno pepper
3 medium size fresh tomatoes, diced
(or a 16 oz can diced tomatoes)
Salt and pepper to taste

Pulse first six ingredients in a food processor until the desired salsa consistency is reached. Dice tomatoes or use canned tomatoes. Combine the chopped mixture with tomatoes. Add salt and pepper to taste and serve.

Makes 1 ½ cups

This is a basic recipe that we use for salsa. Many new combinations can be created from this basic recipe. For example, you can add a clove of garlic, or a couple tablespoons of mayonnaise, substitute lemon juice with lime juice or add cucumbers.

Brie with Green Onions

8 oz of brie
1 cup green onions, finely chopped
1 Tbsp olive oil

Put brie on a small skillet and surround with onions. Sprinkle oil on the onions, cover and cook for about 3 minutes on low heat until the brie becomes just softened. Make sure that the brie does not start melting too much. Turn it over and stir the onions. Allow it to cook for another minute under the cover and remove from heat. When serving, place onions on top of the cheese. Serve with veggies or crackers.

Makes 4 servings

This is a hearty appetizer for cold winter months when you need something quick, warm and filling that can be pre-prepared and cooked quickly at the right moment.

A toast

The Happiest Person on Earth

One wise man was asked about who was the happiest person on earth. "Adam," – answered the wise man. "But why?" – came the stunned response. "He did not have a mother in law!" – explained the wise man. But, I think, that if Adam had such a wonderful mother in law that I have, he would have been a hundred times happier! I drink to my dear mother in law!

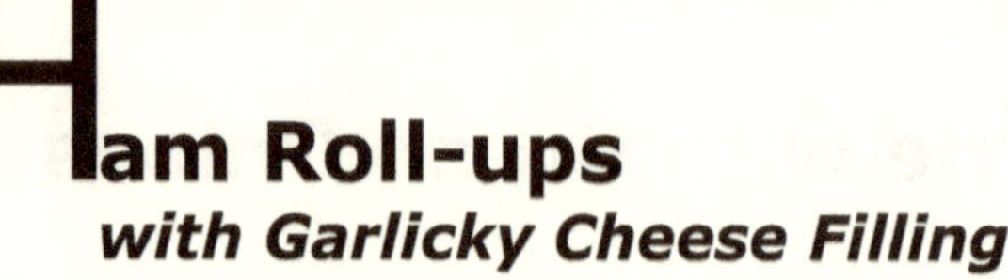

Ham Roll-ups
with Garlicky Cheese Filling

8 oz Gruyère cheese
2 Tbsp mayonnaise
1 large clove garlic
1 Tbsp fresh parsley, finely chopped
½ lb thinly sliced low sodium ham

Finely shred the cheese, add garlic pressed through a garlic press, mayonnaise, parsley and mix well. Cut 2 inch squares out of low salt ham. Put 2 teaspoons of cheese mixture along the side of the ham square, roll into a roll-up and secure with a toothpick. Decorate the plate with parsley.

Makes 4 servings

Guests enjoy these rolls, they are tasty and filling. When we made these rolls for an outside party that was held on the patio facing the ocean, one roll fell off the plate as it was carried to the patio. A fox came over and ate it with an amazing speed! So, this dish is great not only for humans but for foxes as well.

Variations

- Add finely chopped pecans or walnuts to the cheese mixture.
- Use lettuce leaves instead of the ham. It's healthier and adds some crunch to the rolls.

Tuna Sashimi
on a Bed of Avocado

½ lb sashimi grade tuna
1 large avocado
¼ medium size onion
Wasabi
Soy sauce

In a food processor chop onion and the avocado to a uniform smooth paste and spread evenly on a plate.

Mix wasabi with soy sauce to the desired consistency and spiciness. Cut tuna into small cubes. Mix the wasabi with the tuna. Spread the tuna mixture evenly on top of the avocado layer. Serve with cut vegetables or crackers.

Makes 4 servings

There are many recipes for tuna sashimi. My husband invented this one after trying various versions in restaurants. We love this recipe – easy and tasteful.

A superstition
Eating off the Knife

If you have a habit of eating off your knife, you might want to reconsider. Russians believe a person who does this will become angrier over time because of this habit…

Zakuski

Traditional Russian meals start with zakuski, or hors d'oeuvres, which consist of small portions of hot and cold dishes, marinated and smoked fish, accompanied by rye bread and butter, vodka and other beverages. Zakuski are usually crowded on a table, everyone sits down and toasts start.

The word 'zakuski' literally means a bite of something delicious which accompanies a shot of vodka. Without zakuski you miss the full experience as the vodka travels to your stomach and spreads warmth through your body. It's common for Russians to enjoy zakuski for two to three hours before the main course is served.

Zakuski

Beets with Garlic

5 medium size beets (~ 2 lbs)
3 Tbsp mayonnaise
1 large clove garlic
Salt and pepper to taste

Scrub beets well under cold water. Make a cut in each one. Put in a microwave safe pot and cook for 10 to 15 minutes until the beets are cooked through. Shred the beets either by using a hand grater or a food processor. Add garlic pressed through a garlic press and mayonnaise, mix well. Season to taste. Usually no salt is required.

Makes 4 servings

Beets and garlic are used in Russian cooking extensively. This is an easy and extremely tasty recipe that appears on many zakuski tables around Russia.

A toast
I Drink to Your Death

I drink to your death... so that you are buried in a coffin made out of a one hundred year old oak that I planted this morning!

 Smoked Cured Salmon

1 lb of good quality, fatty salmon
1 Tbsp salt
1 tsp sugar or sugar substitute of your choice

Mix salt and sugar in a small bowl. Cover salmon with the salt and sugar mixture. Put most of the mixture on the flesh and just a little bit on the skin. Put salmon skin down on a piece of aluminum foil and wrap it into a package. Put the package on a plate seam up under a heavy press. Leave at room temperature for 4 hours. Salmon will release some juices. After 4 hours, put salmon (still under heavy press) into the refrigerator for another 4 hours or overnight. Rinse with cold water, pat dry and salmon is ready to eat.

Makes 6 servings

Russians love to serve fish as a starter. A regular Russian 'zakuski' table will include several types of smoked fish - hot smoked, cold smoked and cured as this one. Russians usually eat it after a glass of vodka by itself or over white bread with butter. In our family, we serve this salmon in a number of ways – as a zakuska at a starter table, as an appetizer on cucumber slices over cream cheese and for breakfast over a slice of bread with butter.

This is a great 'natural' replacement for a fish oil supplement that is becoming so popular.

Zucchini Caviar

2 Tbsp olive oil
½ cup sweet onion, chopped
2 medium size zucchini
1 stalk of celery, cut into small slices
1 medium size carrot, diced
½ red bell pepper, diced
1 tsp salt
½ tsp jalapeno pepper
3-4 sun dried tomatoes

Sauté onions in a skillet with olive oil until translucent. Add celery, carrots, zucchini and peppers to the skillet, salt the mixture and cook until soft, 3-5 minutes.

When cool enough to handle, transfer the mixture to the food processor, add sun dried tomatoes and pulse a couple of times until just mixed through. Adjust seasoning if needed.

Makes 2 cups

This is a classic Russian appetizer. Its origin is from the southern regions of the former Soviet Union where zucchini and tomatoes grow year round and are plentiful. In the northern regions of Russia, this appetizer is made in big batches in the summer and canned to be enjoyed in the winter.

Variations

- Substitute 1 tomato and ¼ cup of tomato paste instead of sun dried tomatoes. The amount of tomato paste can be increased to up to ½ cup. Make sure that the liquid evaporates before processing in the food processor.

- Substitute jalapeno with regular bell pepper and 2 cloves of garlic.
- Add 1 Tbsp of vinegar.

A toast
A Wiser Perspective

There is an old story about a wise man who could answer seemingly every question that was posed to him. Two boys wanted to trick him. They decided to catch a bird, bring it to the wise man and ask him: "This bird that we are holding, it is alive or dead?" If the old man said it was alive, they would kill it to prove that he was wrong. If he said that it was dead, they would let it fly away.

So they trapped a bird, took it to the wise man and asked him: "Is this bird that we are holding alive or dead?" The old man looked at them and said: "Really, it is in your hands."

This story contains a powerful lesson that there is always another solution when we find the wisdom to look at a situation from a broader perspective. Let's drink to always finding that wiser and higher perspective when we are offered only two choices.

Beet Salad
with Prunes and Nuts

5 medium size beets (~ 2 lbs)
3 Tbsp mayonnaise
1 large clove garlic
5-6 soft pitted prunes
½ cup pecans or walnuts
Salt and pepper to taste

Wash beets well and make a cut in each one. Put in a microwave safe pot and cook covered for 10 to 15 minutes until the beets are cooked through. Shred the beets either by using a hand grater or a food processor. Chop prunes and nuts and add them to beets. Add garlic pressed through a garlic press and mayonnaise, mix well. Season to taste. Usually no salt is required.

Makes 4 servings

This dish is delightful because of the combination of the sweet prunes, crunchy nuts and garlicky flavor. A treat for beet lovers!

Carrot Salad
with Garlic and Mayonnaise

1 lb carrots
3 Tbsp mayonnaise
2 large clove garlic
1 apple

Core and peel the apple, cut into quarters. Shred carrots and apples medium size - not too fine and not too coarse. Add garlic pressed through a garlic press and mayonnaise and mix well. Season to taste. Usually no salt is required.

Makes 4 servings

Root vegetables such as carrots are a staple of Russian cuisine used in salads, main dishes and sweets. In this recipe, carrots can be shredded through a different size grater to achieve a slightly different taste. If shredded finely, the salad will be moister due to the juice released in the process of shredding. Traditionally, the grater size used for this salad is medium.

A toast
To the Present Moment

When you are young, you think that happiness is ahead of you. When you are old, you think that happiness is behind you. How do you ensure that you do not miss your happiness? ... Maybe, the best way is to enjoy the present. Let's drink to the beautiful present moment!

Cheese Salad
with Garlic and Sprats

8 oz Gruyère cheese
2 Tbsp mayonnaise
1 large clove garlic
5-6 sprats

Finely shred the cheese, add garlic pressed through a garlic press, mayonnaise and mix well. Serve the salad mounted in the middle of a platter surrounded by sprats if desired.

Makes 4 servings

This is a filling zakuska that goes well with a shot of vodka. The type of sprats used in Russia come from the Baltic Sea and are smoked and canned by companies in the Baltic republics. Some US supermarkets carry them but Russian stores are more likely to stock them.

A toast
Being a Real Hunter

It became known that one lucky hunter killed a huge tiger in a specific cave. All other hunters rushed to that cave and were also successful. In the meantime, the first hunter killed a great bear in another place. As the other hunters hurried to the new place, the expert hunter tracked a huge leopard to another cave. Who is then the real hunter? The one who finds the pray or the one who follows him? Let's then drink to going our own way and being the real hunter!

Smoked Fish Salad
(Rybnyi Salat)

1 lb of smoked white fish
(or trout or any other smoked fish)
2 eggs boiled, finely chopped
½ cup sweet onion, finely chopped
1 potato boiled or baked in the microwave, diced
3-4 Tbsp mayonnaise

Remove all bones from the fish. Carefully break the fish flesh into small shreds ensuring that there are no bones left. Add the chopped eggs, onion, potato and mayonnaise and mix.

Makes 6 servings

This is a classic Russian zakuska salad. Its origin is from the northern regions of Russia where fish is regularly smoked in smoke houses and placed in storage for winter months. This salad goes well with vodka. It can be served as a starter or as an appetizer on cucumber slices.

Variations

Potato can be substituted by 1 cup of cooked rice. For people who are avoiding starches, the potato or rice can be omitted. They can be substituted with 2 oz of cream cheese or 1 cup of green peas.

Double Cranberry
Molded Salad

1 12 oz bag of cranberries
1 cup sugar
1 large apple
½ cup cranberry juice
2 ¼ oz packages unflavored gelatin

Pour the cranberry juice into a cup, sprinkle gelatin over and let stand until the gelatin softens.

In a food processor pulse cranberries until coarsely chopped. Transfer to a heavy medium saucepan, add sugar and put on low heat until the cranberries release some juice and the sugar starts dissolving. Mix well until the sugar dissolves.

Peel and core the apple and cut into small cubes, add to the berry mixture. Simmer the mixture for 8-10 minutes until cranberries are soft but firm. Remove from heat and add the gelatin mixture.

Spoon cranberry mixture into a decorative mold, cool, cover and refrigerate until firm (at least 4 hours). When ready to serve, soak kitchen towel in hot water, ring out and wrap around the bottom of the mold. Turn the mold on a platter and shake gently until the cranberry mold falls onto the platter. Decorate with parsley.

Makes 4 servings

Cranberry picking is a national pastime in Russia. Cranberries are used extensively in many dishes. This salad is a festive presentation, can be used for Thanksgiving and/or to accompany chicken or other game.

A toast

Making the World a Better Place

One wealthy merchant decided to hide his gold under a tree. He put his gold into a box, dug a hole and buried the box. He returned to take a look at the sacred place almost every day.

A beggar noticed the routine visits and decided to investigate. "Let me go dig up the dirt around the tree and see what's in there", - he reasoned. What a surprise it was when he found the gold! He took out the box and buried a stone instead.

In a couple of days, the merchant came to the tree and decided to dig up his gold to check on it. When he saw the stone instead, he started crying bitterly. The thief came to the merchant and asked: "What's the matter?" "I buried my gold because I did not want to spend it. And now it is gone!"- cried out the merchant.

The thief responded: "Why are you crying? Since you were not going to spend it anyway, why does it matter whether it is the stone or the gold that is buried here?"

Let's drink to those who do not bury their money like a stone but use it to make the world a better place.

Mushrooms Stuffed
with Crab

24 large stuffing mushrooms
1 lb crabmeat
2 oz cream cheese
1 Tbsp mustard
1 Tbsp mayonnaise
2 oz cheddar cheese
¼ tsp salt
¼ tsp cayenne pepper

Remove stems from mushrooms and put into the food processor. You can use a melon baller to remove the stems neatly. Pulse several times to chop the stems coarsely. In a bowl, soften cream cheese with a fork; add chopped stems, mustard, mayonnaise, cheese, salt and pepper. Drain the crabmeat and carefully mix into the cheese mixture until just blended. Stuff mushroom caps with the crab mixture, mounding in center and pressing gently to adhere. Arrange stuffed mushrooms in a buttered baking dish. Position rack in center of oven and preheat to 375°F. Bake until mushrooms are tender about 20-25 minutes.

Makes 6 servings

Russians usually use wild mushrooms and it's hard to find a large number of mushrooms of the same size. So, Russians rarely stuff mushrooms. This recipe is an American adaptation counting on the availability of the same size mushrooms.

Variations

Crabmeat can be substituted by canned tuna fish.

Tomatoes
with Garlicky Cheese

8 oz Gruyere cheese
2 Tbsp mayonnaise
1 large clove garlic
2 Tbsp fresh parsley, finely chopped
6 tomatoes

Finely shred the cheese, add garlic pressed through a garlic press, mayonnaise, and parsley and mix well. Slice tomatoes into ¼ inch rounds and put 2 teaspoons of cheese mixture on each. Sprinkle with parsley.

Makes 4 servings

With colors of red, yellow and green, this dish is a great decorative piece to spice up the zakuski table. Easy to make and a delight to eat!

A superstition
No Empty Bottles on the Table

Having an empty wine or any other alcoholic beverage bottle on the dinner table is considered bad luck in Russia. You will often see empty bottles under the table or under the chairs around the dinner table before they are removed.

Eggplant Caviar
(Baklazhannaya Ikra)

2 Tbsp olive oil
½ cup sweet onion, chopped
½ tsp jalapeno pepper, chopped
1 medium size eggplant, diced
2 Tbsp tomato juice or water
¼ tsp salt
¼ cup fresh cilantro, chopped and packed
¼ cup fresh parsley, chopped and packed
2 cloves of garlic

Sauté onions and jalapeno pepper in skillet with olive oil until onion is translucent. Add eggplant, tomato juice or water and salt. Cover and cook on low heat until soft, about 5 minutes. Turn off the heat and add cilantro, parsley and garlic squeezed through the garlic press. Mix and adjust seasoning if needed.

Makes 6 servings

This is a classic Russian appetizer or a side dish. It is usually pureed to be served as an appetizer. It has been popular in Russia for over 100 years. Its origin is from the southern regions of the Soviet Union. In the Caucasus region and Russia this caviar is spread on top of a piece of rye bread with butter. Great with a shot of vodka!

Variations

Add ½ cup of tomato paste to the eggplant mixture. The resulting dish becomes sweeter and more pungent. Make sure that the liquid evaporates before adding herbs and garlic.

This recipe can serve as a base for a delightful side dish that you can add many other veggies to. Consider adding vegetables such as sweet bell peppers, zucchini, carrot and celery. Carrots and celery should be added with onion, while bell pepper and zucchini with the eggplant.

A toast
To Students of Life

One thief had a student. One day the thief decided to have an exam for his student. He took him to a tree that had a bird's nest and told him: "Steal the eggs but in such a way that the bird is not disturbed."

The student carefully climbed the tree, got close to the nest and was about to grab the eggs when the bird sensed the slight rustling of his clothes and flew away.

The frustrated student descended the tree as his teacher said: "Look how to do it." As soon as the bird was back in the nest, the thief took off his clothes, left them below and quietly as a snake climbed the tree. He was successful in taking the eggs. When he came down, his student and his clothes were
gone.

Let's drink to students of life - all of us
- who surpass their teachers!

Deviled Eggs
with Mushrooms

6 eggs, hard boiled and cut in half horizontally
½ cup sweet onions, chopped
1 Tbsp olive oil
14 oz baby portabella mushrooms, sliced
½ tsp salt
¼ tsp cayenne pepper
2 Tbsp white wine
1 Tbsp mustard
1 Tbsp mayonnaise

Heat a medium size skillet; add olive oil and onions and sauté onions until translucent. Add mushrooms, wine, salt and pepper and cook until mushrooms are soft and there is no liquid left in the skillet.

Separate egg yolks from egg whites. Place egg yolks into the food processor. Add the mushroom mixture, mustard and mayonnaise. Pulse several times until the mixture is smooth. Adjust seasoning. Apportion the mixture among the egg halves. Sprinkle with finely chopped parsley if desired.

Makes 6 servings

Mushrooms are a staple in the Russian cuisine. Picking wild mushrooms is one of the favorite national past times. When picked, mushrooms are then prepared in a number of ways, pickled, cooked and canned or dried to be used later when needed. Every Russian family has a bag of dried mushrooms in the kitchen. When needed, dried mushrooms are soaked in water overnight and then used in soups and other recipes like this one.

Sweet and Sour Beets

2 lb medium size beets
¾ cup white vinegar
½ cup water
⅓ cup sugar
4 black peppercorns
Dill sprigs
Salt

Scrub the beets, make a cut in each and put into a microwavable pan with a lid. Cook in the microwave until tender, about 15 minutes. Rinse in cold water and peel. Cut into rounds about 1/8 thick and put into a glass jar.

Combine vinegar, sugar and water in a small saucepan and bring to a boil. Add salt and pepper to taste. Pour over the beets. Cover and refrigerate overnight.

Makes 8 servings

Pickled beets are very popular in Russia and make a colorful side dish or a salad for the zakuski table.

A toast
To Your Death!

Let's drink to your death but not now, - in a hundred years… So that you do not die naturally but you are murdered. And not just murdered but as a result of jealousy, and not just jealousy but substantiated by fact!

Liver Pate

1 lb beef or chicken liver
1 onion, finely chopped
1 garlic clove
2 large carrots cut in small cubes
2 Tbsp olive oil
3 Tbsp white wine
8 Tbsp (1 stick) unsalted butter
2 Tbsp fresh parsley
2 tsp cognac or brandy
¼ tsp nutmeg
Salt and pepper

Heat a medium size skillet, add olive oil and onion. Cook on low heat until onion is translucent. Add carrots and continue to cook until the carrots are tender.

Rinse liver and dry in paper towels. Cut in small pieces. Melt butter in a medium size skillet, add liver and wine and cook for 10-15 minutes on medium heat until the liver is cooked through but still tender. Add the carrot and onion mixture to the liver and continue to cook for another couple of minutes. Add parsley, salt and pepper.

Transfer the mixture to the food processor, add cognac, nutmeg and process to a pate consistency. Adjust the spices and transfer to a serving bowl. Decorate with parsley.

Makes 2 cups

This dish came to Russia from France. Even though this pate is often served as a part of the zakuski table, many Russians eat this pate for breakfast with coffee spreading it on a layer of butter on a white bread toast.

Olivier
(Russian Salad with Chicken)

8 boiled potatoes in skin
3 large carrots boiled in skin
2 hard boiled eggs
2 15 oz cans green peas
8-10 pickles
2 fresh cucumbers
5 cooked chicken breasts
2 Tbsp fresh parsley
1 onion
1 cup mayonnaise
Salt and pepper to taste

Peel potatoes and carrots and cut into small cubes. Peel the eggs and chop. Cut cucumbers, pickles and chicken breasts into similar size small cubes. Add green peas, parsley and mayonnaise and mix thoroughly.

Makes 8 servings

This is a classic Russian salad which is extremely tasty. It's rare to have a zakuski table without this salad.

Variations

- Add olives cut into thin slices and reduce or eliminate salt.
- Substitute chicken with boiled ham – makes a completely different salad which is also scrumptious.
- Add 1 stalk of celery.

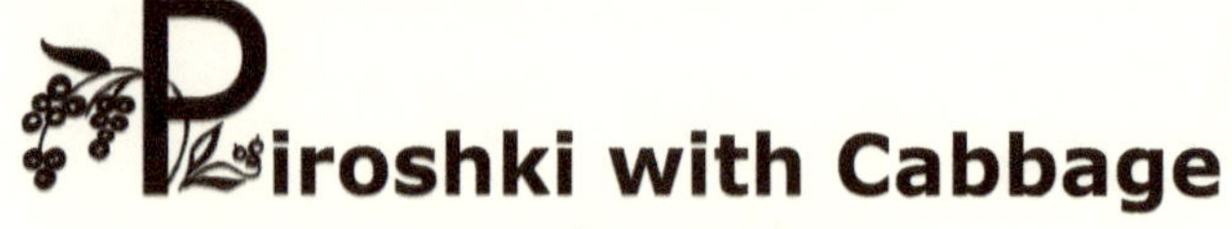

Piroshki with Cabbage

2 lb dough (see Basic Dough recipe)
1 small head of green cabbage
3 Tbsp milk
3 hard boiled eggs
3 Tbsp unsalted butter
1 egg beaten
3 Tbsp fresh parsley, chopped
Salt and pepper to taste

Remove the top leaves from the cabbage head. Cut the cabbage in half, core and slice thinly. Put cabbage into a strainer and pour boiling water on it. Strain well so that no water remains. In a large pot melt the butter, add the cabbage, milk, salt and pepper and cook covered for 10-15 minutes or until the cabbage is tender. When the cabbage cools to room temperature, add chopped eggs and parsley.

Roll the dough on a floured surface and cut rounds 2 inches in diameter with a cup. Put at least one tablespoon of cabbage mixture in the middle of the dough round, close the dough around the filling and pinch the sides of the dough to completely seal the piroshki.

Oil a baking sheet and put piroshki on it with the seam down. Let rest for 10-15 minutes and then brush with the beaten egg. Heat the oven to 350° and bake piroshki for approximately 25 minutes.

Makes approximately 30 piroshki

Basic Dough

2.5 lbs white sifted flour
1 glass milk
3 egg yokes
5 oz sugar
2 Tbsp unsalted butter
2 Tbsp olive oil
2 ¼ oz packages dry yeast
Pinch of salt

Dissolve yeast in warm milk, add sugar, salt, melted butter and oil. Add half of the flour, mix and let stand in a warm place for an hour. After the dough has risen, add egg yokes. Knead the dough adding more flour to make a soft dough. The dough should be smooth but not firm. It will cleanly come off hands. Cover with a towel and let stand for an hour in a warm place. Punch it down and then let it rise for another 15 minutes.

Makes enough dough to make approximately 30 piroshki

Russians are fond of pirogi and piroshki (small, individual portion pirogi). You can find piroshki filled with jam, potatoes, combination of vegetables and other fillings. In the 18th century a piroshki course was a requirement as a part of every dinner menu served at the Russian Tsar's table. And even nowadays most zakuski tables include piroshki.

Vinegret
(Root Vegetable Salad)

2 medium size potatoes
2 medium size carrots
4 medium size beets
1 cup sweet onions, finely chopped
3-4 medium size pickles
2 medium size cucumbers
1 15 oz can small sweet peas
3 Tbsp olive oil
1 Tbsp vinegar
Salt to taste

Scrub all vegetables under running water until clean. Make a cut in each potato and carrot and place into a microwave dish. Cover and microwave until tender. Carrots will cook faster, do not overcook. When done, rinse with cold water and peel. Cook beets in a similar manner in the microwave. They will take longer than potatoes and carrots to cook, about 10 minutes. Rinse with cold water and peel. You might want to wear gloves when you handle beets.

Place chopped onions in small bowl and add vinegar to them. Let stand for a couple of minutes. This will bring out the sweetness in the onions.

Cut root vegetables, pickles, cucumbers into small cubes and combine with onions and strained peas. Add olive oil, mix and season to taste.

Makes 8 servings

This is one of my personal favorite dishes. Its deep color and wonderful taste make me go to the refrigerator several times a day for another bite. The great news is that I can eat as much as I want to without any impact on the waist line – a proven fact.

This dish comes from the middle part of Russia and is common in Ukraine as well. Most Russian families have dachas (small cottages in the country) where they normally grow root vegetables. After the vegetables are harvested in the fall, they are stored in home basements. As a result, an organic, home grown supply of root vegetables is available almost year round for this light but filling salad.

Variations

- Add ½ cup of Kislaya Kapusta (Russian sauerkraut, see separate recipe). Since Kapusta adds sourness and crunch, you might want to reduce the amount of pickles and cucumbers.
- For additional complexity of taste, add one apple, peeled, cored and cut into the same size cubes as the rest of the salad.

A toast
Mohamed and the Mountain

In Russia when someone finally takes a long awaited action they say: "When the mountain does not come to Mohamed, Mohamed goes to the mountain."

In Russia they joke that the mountain never came to Mohamed because he had nothing to drink. Let's drink to our friends who always come to us!

Herring in a Fur Coat

1 herring preserved in salt brine
1 cup sweet onion
1 Tbsp vinegar
3 medium size potatoes
4 medium size carrots
4 medium size beets
3 hard boiled eggs
1 cup mayonnaise

If you buy the herring at a Russian store, you are going to get the whole fish with the head, guts and all. Spread plastic wrap or wax paper on the counter and place the herring on it. Make a cut across the belly and remove the guts. You might want to save the roe, Russians consider it a delicacy. With a quick twist remove and discard the head. Working from inside, flatten the herring so that it is on the counter with its skin down. Carefully remove the middle bone pulling on it from the top of the herring. The middle bone will pull out all the side bones with it as well. You now have two sides of the fish connected with the skin. Pull each half of the herring from the skin. Make sure to remove the spine bones. Make sure that you have no bones left in the flesh. Cut the herring into small cubes.

Follow directions for cooking potatoes, carrots and beets in the Vinegret recipe. Thinly slice onions, put them in a small bowl and add vinegar to them.

Prepare a medium size serving platter. Place herring pieces evenly on the bottom of the platter. Spread onion evenly on top of the herring. Shred potatoes and spread evenly on the layer of herring and onions. Spread a thin layer of mayonnaise on top of potatoes.

Shred carrots and spread evenly on top of the potatoes. Shred beets and spread on top of the carrots. Cover with a thin layer of mayonnaise. Peel and chop eggs and sprinkle on top of the beets.

Makes 8 servings

Russians are in love with herring. It is used in many ways in a variety of dishes. Herring is considered to be a great zakuska for vodka. Some argue that nothing else is needed, just herring. This dish is an ingenious way of using two ingredients beloved by Russians, root vegetables and herring, in a tasty combination. This is an addictive dish even if you do not like beets and herring. Definitely worth trying!

A toast
Sweet versus Bitter

One ruler requested to see his food supply minister and said: "Bring me a dish that is the sweetest in the world." The minister went to the market and bought a beef tongue. The ruler loved the well-prepared dish and lavished praise on the food minister. In a day or two he ordered another dish: "Bring me a dish that is the bitterest in the world." The minister went to the market and bought a beef tongue again. The ruler was confused: "I asked for something bitter and you brought the tongue again. Why?" And the minister explained: "Dear Tsar, there is nothing sweeter in the world than wise words and nothing more bitter than bad words. Everything depends on how we use our tongues." Let's drink to our ability to masterfully control our tongues.

Green Beans Salad
with Potato, Onion and Mustard

1 lb green beans
1 potato
½ large onion
2 Tbsp olive oil
1 Tbsp brown mustard
1 Tbsp balsamic vinegar
1 tsp Worcestershire sauce
¼ cup olive oil
Salt and pepper to taste

Rinse and trim green beans. Cut into one inch pieces. Cook in boiling salted water for approximately 3 minutes. Strain and rinse in cold water to stop the cooking process. Boil potato in its skin or prepare in the microwave. Skin and cut into small cubes. Slice the onion in thin slices and cook in olive oil until tender and slightly browned. Combine beans, potatoes and cooked onion in a bowl, add the mustard dressing, mix, adjust seasoning and serve. Decorate with parsley if desired.

For the mustard dressing – put mustard in a small bowl or a glass and add vinegar and Worcestershire sauce. Slowly add olive oil beating the dressing with a fork. Add salt and pepper to taste.

Makes 4 servings

This is a simple and tasty salad based on the classic Russian combination of ingredients - potato, onion and mustard. Green beans add color and crunch. Enjoy!

![R]ussian Mustard

2 oz dry mustard from a Russian market
½ cup milk
½ tsp salt
¼ tsp sugar
1 Tbsp olive oil
½ tsp vinegar

Put the mustard powder into a jar with a wide lid. Boil the milk. Slowly add milk to the powder mixing well so that no clumps form. The mixture should be of a sour cream consistency. If there is not enough milk, add boiling water until the desired consistency is reached. Add salt and sugar, mix well.

Close the jar tightly and let stand for at least an hour (or overnight) in a warm place. When ready, add vinegar if desired and olive oil.

Makes about 8 oz

Russians use a different type of mustard seed, not the one used in the US and Europe. It belongs to the cruciferous genus and is believed to have been brought to Russia from China. This mustard is VERY SPICY! Be careful smelling it when you open the jar. Taste a tiny amount before you use it liberally as you would any American variety.

When our daughter was small, she invited her friends over to have hot dogs after school. She put this mustard on the table without any warning. When her friends realized how spicy this mustard was, their lunch resulted in a contest full of laughter and tears (from getting too much mustard in one bite).

Mom's Pickled Tomatoes

2 lbs cherry tomatoes
½ onion
½ green bell pepper
3 cloves of garlic
1 quart water
1 tsp salt
4 tsp sugar
1 Tbsp vinegar
1 bay leaf
Dill sprigs
4 black peppercorns

Arrange tomatoes, peeled and cut into slivers garlic, onion cut in rings and slices of green pepper in a jar with a wide lid. Boil water and pour into the jar with the vegetables. Pour the water out of the jar into a saucepan. You just blanched the vegetables and measured the amount of water needed to fill the jar.

Bring the strained water back to a boil. Add salt, sugar, peppercorns, bay leaf, dill sprigs and vinegar and simmer for 10 minutes. Pour back into the jar together with the spices. Cover tightly, cool and store in the refrigerator.

Makes 1 jar (4 cups or 1 liter size)

This recipe is from my Mom. My parents used to grow tomatoes at their dacha and prepare them this way. They usually made more than they could use and my entrepreneurial Mom used to sell them in a farm market every fall. This is another popular and colorful zakuska that goes well with a shot of vodka.

Lecho
(Bell Peppers in Tomato Sauce)

1 lbs red bell peppers
1 lb carrots
1 lb onions
1 ½ lbs fresh tomatoes
1 cup olive oil
½ cup vinegar
1 cup sugar
Salt and pepper

Cut peppers into strips. Chop onions and shred carrots. Combine all ingredients in a large heavy saucepan, bring to a boil and cook on low heat for 40 minutes. Adjust seasoning. Transfer the mixture into jars while piping hot, close the lids tightly and let cool. Store in the refrigerator. This mixture can store for several months.

Makes 3 (1 liter) jars

My Mom used to make Lecho every fall when the vegetables were plentiful. We always had this delicious dish in the refrigerator to our delight and the delight of drop in guests.

A superstition
Whistling in the House

Russians will tell you to never whistle in the house. They warn that if you do, you might never become wealthy.

Klyukovka
(Sasha's Cranberry Vodka)

Vodka, Smirnoff or any other type
1 cup cranberries
1 ½ tsp sugar
2 tsp frozen raspberries, thawed

Prepare one quart size jar with a wide lid. Chop cranberries and raspberries with sugar in a food processor or a blender to a fine consistency. Put the mixture into the jar (it should fill about one sixth of the jar volume). Fill the jar with vodka and close the lid tightly.

Let stand at room temperature for 3 days shaking the jar once a day. Strain through a cheese cloth and make sure to wring the solids dry. Pour vodka into a bottle preferably with a screw top and store in the freezer.

Makes 1 (0.75 liter) bottle

This recipe was created by our friend, Sasha Livshin, who has been making this vodka at home for many years to the enjoyment of all his friends and relatives. He usually brings a bottle with him when he visits. No wonder he is welcome everywhere!

A tradition
Russian Vodka

It is a common belief that Russians love vodka. For the most part it is true and most Russian families have a bottle in the freezer at all times. Vodka is served cold. The process of drinking it is simple: exhale, drink, inhale and have some 'zakuski'.

Russian history is full of great events where vodka played a major role. Ivan the Terrible used it as a 'Russian weapon' to soften foreigners while negotiating trade agreements with them. In his times vodka was regarded as a ceremonial drink.

Among the people, vodka is loved for making people kinder, more open and happy. It is also considered to be a 'devil's drink'. In the 16th century drunkenness became a real issue in the country. Peter the Great complained that more men were killed by vodka than by enemy bullets. However, he himself was known to start his day with a quarter of a liter of vodka seasoned with black pepper. He was also the one who created a whole network of vodka factories and bars around Russia. The profits were used to build the fleet and wage the war against Sweden.

Statisticians report that Russians spend around 9% of their income on vodka. There are over 150 brands ranging from 40 to 70 percent proof. Vodka is also used in Russia as a sophisticated remedy and for many other purposes. Wrapping the chest in vodka soaked towels is an ancient Russian remedy for influenza, or around the neck – remedy for tonsillitis. Vodka mixed with sunflower oil makes an excellent wood furniture polish. And on and on it goes…

Mimosa Salad

2 cans sardines packed in oil (3.75 oz each)
1 onion, finely chopped
3-4 hard boiled eggs
4 Tbsp unsalted sweet butter
8 oz Swiss cheese
3 Tbsp mayonnaise
Green onions and fresh parsley, finely chopped

Peel eggs, cut in half and separate whites from yokes. Chop egg whites in a food processor. Mash egg yolks with a fork in a small bowl into a fine paste. Mash sardines with a fork in a small bowl. Make sure that the butter is really cold. Shred it on a large shredder. Separately shred the cheese on a large shredder.

On a small serving platter carefully layer the ingredients in the following order fluffing each layer with a fork: egg whites, onions, half of the fish mixture, mayonnaise, parsley, butter, the remaining fish mixture, cheese, mayonnaise, egg yolks, onions and herbs.

Makes 4 servings

This is a fancy presentation of a savory combination of cheese, fish and eggs. Scrumptious!

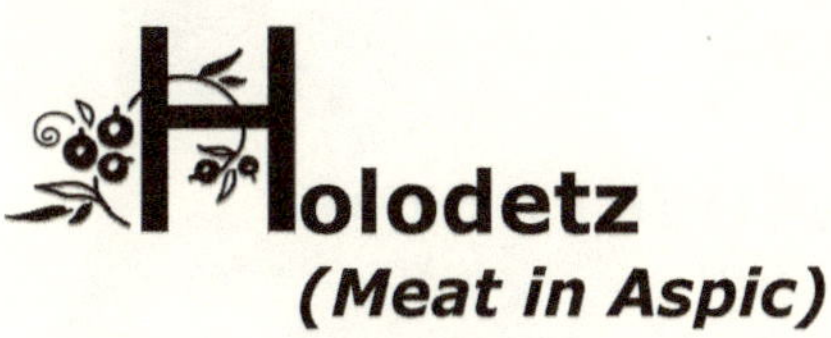olodetz
(Meat in Aspic)

2 small foreleg pork knuckles
3 ½ lbs beef and pork meat with bones
3 quarts water
1 onion peeled
3 bay leaves
5 black peppercorns
2 garlic cloves
1 carrot and 1 celery stalk for decorating
Salt

Place the meat and bones into a pot with water, bay leaves, onions and peppercorns. Bring to boil and skim off the foam. Simmer for about 3 hours. When the liquid has reduced to about a third, add salt and simmer for another 15 minutes. Remove from heat, strain the stock, remove the bones and separate the meat into small pieces.

In a separate small pot boil carrots and celery for decorating. Arrange meat in a large terrine. Cut vegetables into rounds or other decorative shapes and arrange on top of the meat. Add garlic pressed through a garlic press to the stock and pour the stock over the meat. Put the terrine in a cool place to set for 4 hours or overnight. Serve with horseradish.

Makes about 8 oz

Since meat was a delicacy in Soviet Russia, families saved meat bones and meat for major holidays. This classic dish was normally reserved for major holidays and was always welcome at the zakuski table. Many toasts were followed by a bite of this delightful dish!

Marinated Mushrooms

2 lbs of white mushrooms, or any other variety
2 cups water
1 cup vinegar
1 tsp salt
2 bay leaves
12 black peppercorns
8 cloves
¼ cup sugar

Clean mushrooms with wet paper towels. Prepare marinade by bringing all the rest of the ingredients to a boil and simmering for 3 minutes.

Bring a pot of salted water to a boil, add mushrooms and cook for 5-10 minutes. If working with wild mushrooms, strain the first batch of water. Bring another batch of salted water to a boil and cook mushrooms again for 5 minutes. Strain and put into sterilized glass jars. Add marinade. Close lids tightly and turn the jars over on their lids on the counter to ensure tight seal. Store jars in the refrigerator. These mushrooms can be stored for at least a month.

Makes 1 (one liter) jar

In Russia this is a must for a zakuski table. Mushrooms, especially the wild variety, usually disappear quickly after the first couple of toasts.

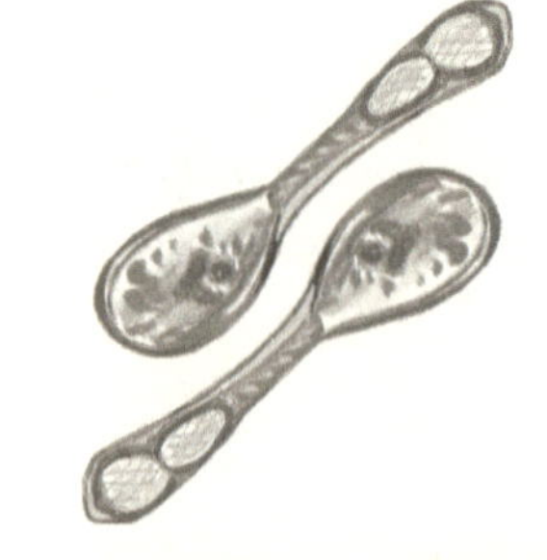

Kislaya Kapusta
(Russian Sauerkraut)

5 lb green cabbage
4 large carrots
1 cup cranberries
2 tart apples such as Granny Smith
Salt

Shred cabbage and put it into a large bowl. Combine with shredded carrots and add salt. Use your hands to mix with movements similar to kneading dough. This kneading ensures that the cabbage releases some juice. Core and slice apples into 8 slices each. Add to cabbage. Add cranberries and mix. Let stand for an hour or so to get more juices released.

Transfer cabbage into a glass jar with a wide mouth or a tall bucket. The cabbage should be submerged in its juices. Add water if necessary. Put a small saucer on top of the cabbage and put a weight on it (such as another jar filled with water). Cover with a towel and place in a cool place for four days.

Every day, remove the weight and clean out any foam that might develop on top of the cabbage. Using a long knife, pierce the cabbage through to the bottom of the jar to release the gases. Make sure that the cabbage is submerged in liquid. If not, add some water to cover. Keep the cabbage in a cool place until it is fully fermented - up to 10 days. After it is done, transfer to individual sterilized jars. It will keep in the refrigerator for up to 3 months. Serve as a side salad sprinkled with olive oil.

Makes about 2 quart jars

This dish is a staple of Russian cuisine. Almost every Russian family has this delight stored in their refrigerators, garages or basements in the winter. This cabbage does not taste anything like the sauerkraut that you can buy in the supermarket. In contrast, Kapusta is crunchy and tasty. Any Russian market in the US sells this cabbage.

A toast
Sing Me Your Song

A long time ago there lived many poets in a small kingdom. They walked the streets and sang their songs. The ruler of the kingdom loved to listen to the songs when he was not busy. But once he heard a song that talked about the brutality of the Ruler, about his greediness and unfairness. The Ruler got really angry and ordered that the author of the dreadful song be found immediately.

However, after much search the author of the song could not be found. The Ruler then ordered to find all poets, bring them to the capital and imprison them. The guards rushed across the kingdom, found every poet and every singer and put them all in prison.

In the morning, the Ruler came to talk to the poets: "Now, I'd like everyone to sing me one of their songs." All poets in turn sang their songs. They were songs of praise of the Ruler's bright mind, his loving heart, his beautiful wives, his wisdom and power. They sang the words of praise - that there has not lived such a wonderful and fair Ruler than the current one until now. The Ruler listened and let each one of the poets go free.

At some point only three poets were left who refused to sing any songs. They were thrown back into prison. Everyone thought that the Ruler forgot about them.

The Ruler came to see them in three months. He told the three poets: "Sing me a song." One of the three started singing immediately. The song was about the wisdom, the mightiness and the power of the Ruler. The poet was let go. The other two poets refused to sing.

The other two poets were taken to a big fire that was laid out on the city square. "You will burn if you do not sing me a song," – he told the two poets. One of the poets broke down and started singing. His song was about the great Ruler, his wonderful qualities and wisdom. The Ruler let the poet go.

Only one poet was left who refused to sing. "Tie him to the pole and start the fire," – ordered the Ruler. The order was executed. A couple of minutes later the poet started singing the very song that had started the whole story – the song about the cruelty, the unfairness and the greediness of the Ruler. "Take him off the pole immediately!" – cried out the Ruler. "I do not want to lose the only real poet in my country!" Let's drink to the great art of telling the truth even in the face of death.

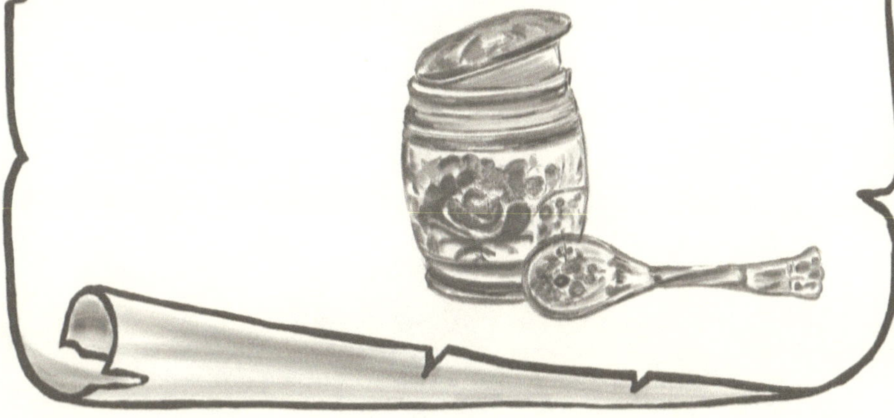

Main Dishes

In Russia, by the time main dishes arrive at the table, guests have had a number of drinks and many satisfying zakuski. As a result, it is a challenge to serve more food and create a main course that guests devour. This section includes many savory delights that will please your guests and keep the flow of toasts going.

Usually many zakuski dishes are left on the table, just pushed to the sides, so that the main course can be placed in the middle of the table, expanding the feast. This can prove to be surprisingly difficult!

Main Dishes

Roast Duck

1 duck
Salt

Cut the duck: first cut out the back spine and then cut the two halves into 3 pieces, the leg, the middle part and the wing. Cut off the extra fat and reserve. Punch the skin with a fork. Salt the pieces.

Prepare a cast iron pot where the duck will be roasted. Preheat the oven to 425°F. In the meantime, heat a large skillet, put the duck pieces skin down on the skillet and brown them until golden brown. While browning, transfer extra fat from the skillet into the cast iron pot. Arrange the pieces in the pot skin up. Cut the reserved fat into small pieces and arrange around the duck pieces. Roast the duck for 1 hour periodically basting it with juices and fat. Reduce the temperature to 375°F or 400°F depending on the extent the duck has cooked to this point and cook for another 30 minutes or so until the duck is extremely tender and comes off the bones easily.

In the classic Russian recipe this duck is served with potatoes. Potatoes are usually cut into 3-4 pieces each and browned in a skillet on high heat, salted and then added to the duck 20-30 minutes before the end of cooking. The duck also goes well with Tushenaya Kapusta – Braised Cabbage (see a separate recipe).

Makes 6 servings

This recipe produces the best duck that you have ever tasted! When my husband was young, he could eat the whole duck! I always marveled at this fact. When we serve this duck, there is usually nothing left…

A tradition
An Evening with Tamada

Tamada means 'a master of ceremonies'. The word and the tradition come from Georgia where any celebration has a tamada. Tamada's role is to orchestrate the party by eloquent interventions and to ensure that everyone has a great time. The process is often raised to an art form. Tamada is an honorary title. Usually an older person with a rich life experience is selected to lead the celebration. In each country and for each type of celebration there is a tradition to the sequence of toasts that are raised.

Many toasts in this book are stories, but toasts can also be eloquent expressions of a point. Tamada is a master of this skill. For example: "Wine is an agent against grief, but it is not an agent to reduce melancholy. This is why I am now drinking to life. There is much in the world that is beautiful: the strength of the oxen, the dew in the morning, the richness of the earth, the pressing of wine, the smile of a pretty woman, the heart of a knight. But the most beautiful of all is the growth of a new generation. To life and to children."

The main objective behind the toasts and the tamada's role is to praise the characteristics of the people present. This is why everyone leaves parties in Russia fortified and happy.

Pelmeni
(Siberian Meat Filled Dumplings)

DOUGH
1 lb wheat flour
1 egg
1 cup VERY cold water

MEAT FILLING
½ lb ground beef
½ ground lamb
½ ground pork
1 onion
1 garlic clove
2 cups water
Salt and pepper

Sift the flour into a mound on a clean surface. Make a dent in the middle of the mound. Break the egg into the dent. Using your hands mix the egg into the flour working from the middle of the flour mound to the sides. Add water in batches to the middle of the mound making sure that it does not leak on the sides. Mix the water into the flour until the dough is smooth and elastic. Wrap the dough into a towel and put aside for 30 minutes, it will become more elastic.

In a bowl combine all ground meats. Put onion and garlic into the food processor and chop into a paste. Add to the meats. Add salt and pepper. Mix with your hands, adding small amounts of

water until the mixture becomes smooth. It will easily stay in a large ball.

Making pelmeni: Cut a piece of dough and make a long roll about ½ inch in diameter. Cut the roll into small rounds about ¼ inch. Sprinkle flour on the table and roll each little piece of dough into a very thin wrapper, a little more than an inch in diameter. Put 1 teaspoon of meat stuffing on each wrapper, fold in half and tightly pinch the sides. Connect the two sides of the pelmeni together making it into a round shape, pinch the corners together well. Put prepared pelmeni on a cutting board sprinkled with flour and put into the freezer. When frozen, store pelmeni in a tightly sealed plastic bag in the freezer. Pelmeni can store in the freezer for at least a month.

To cook, boil salted water, add a bay leaf and a couple of peppercorns. Add pelmeni to the boiling water and ensure that they do not stick to the bottom. Pelmeni are ready when they rise to the top. Remove pelmeni with a slotted spoon. Serve accompanied by butter, sour cream, vinegar, ketchup and liquid in which pelmeni were cooked.

Makes 100+ pelmeni (about 8 servings)

When you start eating pelmeni, it's hard to stop. Many Russians can easily eat 30-40 in one meal. Some can eat over 50! Our family occasionally has pelmeni parties with friends and co-workers at which we get together, sit around and talk while making these delicious bundles. Then we have fun cooking them and finding the special ones that each one of us made in a special manner. Total fun!

In Siberia, pelmeni are stored in bags outside the windows in the winter since it is SO cold there. Across Russia most families have pelmeni in their freezers. It's a great treat on a night when you are not in the mood for cooking.

Plov
(Roasted Lamb with Rice)

1 leg of lamb
1 onion, chopped
2 carrots cut in small cubes
2 cups of rice
4 ½ cups of water
¾ tsp salt
1 bay leaf
1 Tbsp fresh parsley, chopped

Remove bones from a leg of lamb, remove extra fat and cube the meat into ½ inch cubes. Cut fat into small pieces and cook on low heat in a small skillet transferring released fat into the iron pot where the lamb will be cooked.

Heat a cast iron pot with the accumulated fat to a high temperature and brown lamb cubes. Add carrots, onion, salt, pepper and the bay leaf. Roast lamb in the oven at 425°F for 45 minutes to 1 hour stirring occasionally. There should not be much liquid left in the pot.

Add rice, water and salt to the lamb. Mix and return to the oven.

Decrease the temperature to 400°F and cook for another 20 minutes. There should not be any liquid left in the pot. Add additional cooking time until the liquid is totally absorbed by the rice. Add parsley, fluff the rice and serve.

Makes 8 servings

Variations

In Azerbaijan this dish is also prepared with dry fruit and spices. In the above recipe add the following dry fruits to the meat with the rice.

- 1 cup raisins.
- 1 ½ cups dried apricots.
- ½ pitted prunes.

Plov is the national dish of Azerbaijan where rice is known as the 'people's second bread'. Plov is a classic dish that has been and is still extremely popular across the Middle Asian states of the former Soviet Union. It comes in many variations and flavors. Some basic recipes do not even include meat, just rice and spices. Saffron is often used to spice plov. In our family plov is usually served with a tomato salad (Tomato and Onions or Tomato and Arugula, see separate recipes).

A toast
Facing Challenges

There is a fairy tale bird called the Phoenix that has a wondrous ability to burn and then recreate itself from its ashes. I want to wish you this ability - so that regardless of the challenges we face we can bounce back as the Phoenix does. To your strength and courage!

amb
with Roasted Vegetables

1 leg of lamb
1 eggplant
2 medium size zucchini
2 red bell peppers
1 large onion
3 Tbsp olive oil
2 cloves garlic
1 bay leaf
Salt and pepper

Remove bones from a leg of lamb, remove extra fat and cube the meat into ½ inch cubes. Cut fat into small pieces and cook on low heat in a small skillet transferring released fat into the cast iron pot where the lamb will be cooked.

Heat the iron pot with the accumulated fat to a high temperature and brown lamb cubes. Add salt, pepper and the bay leaf. Roast lamb at 425°F for 1 hour stirring occasionally.

Cut the eggplant, zucchini, and bell peppers into similar size cubes. Slice the onion. Combine these ingredients with olive oil, salt and pepper and mix. Add veggies to the pot with lamb and mix.

Decrease the temperature to 400°F and cook for another 20 minutes. Do not overcook. The vegetables should be tender but firm. Add garlic pressed through the garlic press, parsley, mix and serve.

Makes 8 servings

This is a variation on Plov, replacing rice with vegetables for people who prefer to stay away from carbohydrates. It is not a replacement for Plov, however, the two dishes are completely different in character and taste. This lamb can be served with a regular salad with a zesty dressing.

A toast
Riding a Donkey is Not a Simple Affair

Once upon a time a farmer and his son had to travel to the nearest village. The farmer decided to walk and mounted his son on their donkey. Soon they met a group of people and one of them said: "Look, the old person is walking and the young guy is riding the donkey." The farmer decided to ride the donkey and asked his son to walk. Soon they met a large group of people. One of them looked at the farmer and his son and said: "Look at that! This huge person is riding the donkey and the poor little guy is dragging along." The farmer dismounted the donkey, let the donkey go first and he and his son walked behind. They walked for awhile and met another group of people. One of them said: "Look at this! The donkey is without a rider and these two are beating the road." The farmer and his son mounted the donkey together. They rode for a little while and met another group. These people started laughing: "Look at these two. The poor donkey is almost dying carrying the two of them." The farmer and his son dismounted the donkey. The farmer decided to carry the donkey, saying: "It seems that this is the only way that I can get rid of the cruel tongues of these people."

Let's drink to us paying no attention to the peoples' opinions and pursuing our own path!

Chicken Kiev

4 large chicken breasts
2 cups bread crumbs
8 Tbsp sweet butter
2 large eggs
Salt and pepper
2-4 cups of canola oil

Cut chicken breasts in half. Put each breast between two layers of plastic wrap and pound to a thin cutlet. Salt and pepper each cutlet.

Break eggs onto a plate and beat lightly with a fork. Put bread crumbs onto another plate. Put a piece of butter onto each cutlet, fold the sides of the cutlet around the butter and roll it into a roll as tightly as possible. Dip the cutlet into the egg mixture and then into the breadcrumbs making sure that all seams are sealed with egg and breadcrumbs. Repeat with the egg and the breadcrumbs. Put prepared cutlets onto another plate, seam down, and transfer into the freezer to seal.

Heat ½ inch of oil in a pot that is deep enough to hold 2-4 cutlets. Slowly put the cutlets into the oil, seam down and cook until a golden crust forms. Turn them over and cook until the whole cutlet is browned to a nice golden color – 4-5 minutes each side. Remove from oil and put in a baking dish and into an oven heated to 250°F to keep the cutlets warm while cooking the remaining cutlets.

Makes 4 servings

A toast
Taming Tigers

This story happened in a country in the tropics. One daughter complained to her mother about her husband who had been cheating on her. Her mother listened to her and said: "This is something that is fixable. Please bring me two hairs from a tiger's whiskers. "This is impossible," – said the frightened daughter with alarm. "Try it, you are a woman, you should be able to do anything."

The daughter thought about the task long and hard. Then she slaughtered a lamb, cut a piece of meat and went into the forest. She hid in the bushes and waited for a tiger. When a tiger came, it charged at her. The daughter threw the meat at the tiger and ran away. Next day she came to the same place with another piece of meat. When the tiger charged, she threw the meat to him but did not run. She stayed and looked at how he ate. On the third day, the tiger was waiting for her and appeared friendly. The woman offered the meat in the cups of her hands and the tiger took it. On the fourth day the tiger ran to her, ate the meat and put his head on her lap and fell asleep. The woman let him go deeper into sleep and then pulled two hairs from his whiskers and brought them home to her mother.

"See now," said the mother, "you tamed a wild animal such as a tiger. Go and tame your husband with either cunning or love. Remember, there is a tiger in every man." Let's drink to the women who can tame the tigers in us!

Roast Boned Turkey
with Deluxe Stuffing

1 whole turkey, 8 to 10 lbs
2 lb sausage meat
3 eggs
1 cup sour cream
2 Tbsp chopped fresh parsley
Salt
½ lb thinly sliced boiled ham
½ lb thinly sliced cooked tongue
3 thin slices liver sausage (can be omitted)
3 hard boiled eggs
1 cup dry white wine
¼ cup shelled pistachio nuts

Veal Mousse
1 lb ground veal
2 eggs
1 cup light cream
Salt and pepper

Wash and dry the turkey and bone it (see Boning Poultry). Spread the boned turkey, skin side down on a clean kitchen counter. Mix the sausage meat, eggs, sour cream, herbs and salt and pepper. Spread on the turkey. Mix ground veal with eggs, add salt and pepper. Use a small wire whisk to beat in the cream. Spread the veal mousse on the sausage mixture. Cover the mousse with the slices of ham, tongue and liver sausage. Place the eggs in a row down the middle of the spread turkey. Scatter pistachio nuts over the surface.

Lift the sides of the turkey carefully and roll to the center. Sew the back seam with a thread. Reshape the bird so that it is the shape of the original bird as much as possible. Place the bird in a roasting pan and roast at 375° for 10 minutes per pound, basting with a mixture of wine and water every 20 minutes.

To serve, remove the strings. Cut slices and arrange on a serving platter slightly overlapping so that the design of the stuffing is displayed.

Makes 8 servings

This is our family's special occasion turkey that we usually prepare for the Thanksgiving feast. It is wonderfully tasty and festive. It is usually met with WOWs from guests who have not seen it before. If you'd like to WOW your guests, this recipe is worth the time investment.

Variations

The following vegetarian mixtures can replace the sausage or veal stuffing, or both, with a layer of ham and tongue in-between.

- Mushroom Ragu (see separate recipe).
- Bell Peppers with Dill (see separate recipe).

A superstition
If You Want to Keep a Friend

Russians avoid hugging someone, especially friends, in a doorway because it is believed that you may part with the person and this parting maybe forever. They will either step out into the hallway or into the room to give the person a hug.

Boning Poultry

This procedure applies to the boning of all poultry – turkey, chicken, duck, pheasant, quail and others. In the following procedure we will use turkey as an example.

1. Clean and wash the turkey. Dry thoroughly with paper towels. Cut off the wings between the shoulder and the elbow. Cut off the tail. Place the turkey breast side down on a clean counter or on a cutting board.

2. With a small sharp knife cut a slit through the skin down the center of the back of the turkey along the whole length. Proceed to bone one side of the turkey and then the other side according to the following steps, making sure not to puncture the skin.

3. Slip the knife carefully under the skin of the lower bony part of the back and cut off the meat that is there over the bone. Then edge the knife along the ribs and loosen the breast meat. Be careful not to cut the skin at the breastbone where it is attached with a very thin membrane.

4. Work the knife through the thigh joint and detach the leg from the body.

5. Cut through the knee joint and separate the drumstick from the thigh.

6. Cut through the meat of the thigh through to the bone, down the length of the thigh. Cut the bone away from the meat.

7. Either chop the knobs of the drumsticks or cut the skin around them so that you can pull the drumstick bone from the inside.

8. Pull the skin away from the drumstick. With the back of the knife peel the drumstick bone away from the meat.

9. Pull the skin away from the shoulder. With the knife tip detach the wing joint. Then with the knife tip peel the wing bone away from the meat.

10. One side of the turkey is now completely boned. It should be attached to the carcass only by the skin at the center of the breastbone. Leave it there for now. Bone the other side of the turkey.

11. When both sides are boned, hold the carcass away from the meat and skin. The carcass is now attached only by the thin skin at the breastbone. Carefully, cut the skin away from the breastbone, down the center.

12. Congratulations, you have completed the boning process! Spread out the turkey skin side down and proceed with the stuffing.

This procedure is quite a challenge, especially the first time. However, when you do it several times, it becomes easy. You can become an expert at it and create wonderful dishes by stuffing chicken and other poultry with ease. Think of a boned chicken with spinach and feta, for example. A sheer delight!

Beef Stroganov

2 lbs beef tips or beef tenderloin
2 Tbsp olive oil
¼ cup chicken or beef stock
2 Tbsp white wine
1 small onion, peeled and quartered
½ cup sour cream
Salt and pepper
1 bay leaf

Cut the meat into thin strips against the grain. Heat a large skillet until really hot, add olive oil and brown meat on both sides in batches, transferring the browned beef into a pot.

Add chicken or beef stock along with the wine to the skillet while it is still hot, mix with the remaining juices from the meat and add the liquid to the pot. Add onion pieces to the pot, bury them in the meat. Add the bay leaf and make sure that it is immersed in the liquid.

Simmer on low heat for 45 min or so making sure that there is enough liquid in the pot. When meat is tender, add sour cream, mix, simmer for another 3 minutes or so, add salt and pepper to taste.

Makes 6 servings

The origin of this dish is French. It is believed to have been invented by a French cook who worked for Count Alexander Stroganov (1795-1891) in Odessa. Interestingly, he was not even much of a gourmet but liked to entertain. The dish became known because it was served in small portions at his many parties.

Chicken Wings

4 lbs chicken wings
1 cup orange or grapefruit juice
2 Tbsp olive oil
1 Tbsp Tabasco sauce
1 tsp dry garlic
1 tsp dry onion
1 tsp dry parsley

If you get uncut chicken wings, cut off the thin ends and then cut the remainder in half. Discard the ends or use them for preparing chicken broth. Salt the wing parts and put into a buttered baking dish.

Combine the rest of the ingredients in a bowl and then pour the sauce onto the wings. Bake at 375°F for 40 minutes covered and 10 min uncovered under the broiler, mixing them occasionally to get them browned.

Makes 6 servings

These wings can be served as an appetizer, especially for a party. Or as a main dish for a homey dinner.

A toast
Are You Sick?

He is not drinking with us… this means that he is sick. Let's drink to his health!

Vareniki
(Filled Dumplings)

2 cups flour
2 eggs
1 Tbsp olive oil
8 Tbsp water

FARMER'S CHEESE FILLING
2 cups farmer's cheese
1 egg
½ Tbsp sugar
Pinch of salt

POTATO FILLING
3 large potatoes
1 large onion
3 Tbsp sweet unsalted butter
2 oz cheddar cheese
Salt and pepper

CHERRY FILLING
2 cups pitted canned cherries
1 Tbsp sugar
1 tsp cornstarch
1 Tbsp cherry liqueur

Make a mound of flour on a clean surface. Make a dent in the middle. Beat eggs with a fork in a bowl and add half a teaspoon of salt. Pour some of the eggs mixture into the dent and mix with the flour in the middle of the mound with your hands. Continue mixing the eggs into the flour, then do the same with olive oil, then the water. Knead until the dough is smooth, at least 3 minutes. Cover with a linen towel and let stand for 30 minutes or so.

Cut a piece of dough and make a long roll about ½ inch in diameter. Cut the roll into small rounds about ¼ inch each. Sprinkle flour on the table and roll each little piece of dough into a very thin wrapper, a little more than an inch in diameter. Put 1 teaspoon of the filling on each wrapper, fold in half and tightly pinch the sides. Connect the two sides of the vareniki together, making it into a round shape, then pinch the corners together well. Put prepared vareniki on a surface sprinkled with flour. Vareniki can be frozen and will store well for at least a month

Bring salted water to a boil in a large pot. Carefully lower vareniki into the water with a slotted spoon. Cook for 5-7 minutes until vareniki float to the surface. Carefully remove with a slotted spoon. Serve with sour cream.

Farmer's cheese filling: Combine all ingredients, mix well.

Potato filling: Fry chopped onions in butter until golden. Peel, boil in salted water and mash potatoes. Combine with onions and cheese.

Cherry filling: Drain cherries and reserve the syrup. Mix cherries with sugar to taste. Mix in the cornstarch. Fill each varenik with 4 cherries making sure to seal well. Boil the syrup down to one cup, add liqueur. This sauce can be served on the side along with the sour cream.

Makes 4 servings (about 50 vareniki)

Vareniki originate in Ukraine. They are made with simple noodle dough and can be filled with anything you can create. The most common fillings are farmer's cheese, potato and cherries.

Blini
(Russian Thin Pancakes)

½ cup flour
¼ Tbsp salt
1 egg
1 tsp baking powder
½ cup milk
½ cup water
Olive oil
Sweet unsalted butter

Combine flour and salt in a medium size bowl. Lightly beat the egg, then add to the flour and mix. Combine milk and water in a glass. Add this liquid to the flour in bathes making sure to mix well each time.

Heat a small skillet, add olive oil and pour about an eight of a cup for each pancake. Make sure that the pancake mixture covers the bottom of the skillet in a thin layer. Cook for 1-2 minutes and turn over. Cook for another 1-2 minutes. Transfer to a hot plate and spread butter over the top of the pancake. To fill blini, put filling on the side of blini and wrap into an envelope shape. Brown both sides of the filled blini in the skillet.

Makes 8 blini

Meat filling: Sauté half an onion, chopped, until translucent, add ½ lb of ground meat, salt and cook until ready.

Farmer's cheese filling: Combine ½ cup of farmer's cheese, one egg and 1 Tbsp sugar. Mix well to an even consistency.

A wedding tradition
Ransom for the Bride

The groom comes to the bride's home with his closest friends and relatives. To get the bride he has to pay ransom to the group on the bride's side. Everything is played out as a joke and both sides are competing in the sense of humor. After getting the bride, the couple gets out of the house into the limousine to go to the marriage ceremony.

Racing to the Carpet

In a traditional Orthodox wedding ceremony the bride and the groom must stand on a special carpet as they recite their marriage vows, but first they race each other to it. Whoever reaches the carpet first will, presumably, be the head of the household.

A toast
An Offering of Bread and Salt to Newlyweds

Traditionally the parents of the bride open the wedding celebration with the offering of bread and salt with a recent addition of wine: "We offer you bread and salt as symbols of health, prosperity and long life. Bread... so that your house may never know hunger. Salt... so that your life may always have flavor. And wine... so that joy and prosperity may reign forever."

Golubtsi
(Stuffed Cabbage)

1 head green cabbage
1 lb ground beef
½ lb ground pork
2 medium size onions
3 cloves garlic
½ lb cooked rice
1 bunch of fresh parsley
1 bunch of fresh dill
1 cup water
1 carrot
1 medium size tomato
4 Tbsp olive oil
1 cup heavy cream
1 cup shredded cheddar cheese
Salt and pepper

Remove outside leaves from the cabbage and core it. Boil salted water in a large pot and submerge the cabbage in it. Cook for 2-3 minutes at the most. Remove cabbage from the water and let cool.

Peel onion and garlic and finely chop in the food processor. In a mixing bowl combine ground beef, pork, the onion mixture, rice, chopped parsley and dill. Add salt and pepper. Add water in batches and mix well.

Separate the cabbage head into individual leaves. Either crush the stem side of the leaves or cut the thick part out with a knife. Put 1-2 tablespoons at the base of each leaf, fold in the sides and roll tightly tucking the sides tightly as you roll. Heat olive oil in a skillet and brown golubtsi on both sides, starting with the seam side, 3 minutes per side. Transfer to a casserole dish.

For the sauce, sauté chopped onions until translucent, add diced carrots and cook until done. Add heavy cream, salt and pepper. Bring to a boil and add tomatoes. Boil for 5 minutes until the sauce thickens slightly. Add parsley and dill. Pour the sauce over golubtsi in the casserole dish. Cook for 15 minutes at 350°. Sprinkle with cheese. Cook for another 10 minutes until the top brown to a golden color. Serve with the sauce that golubtsi were cooked in and sour cream. Garnish with parsley.

Makes 6 servings

This is a familiar Eastern European classic. It is popular throughout Russia but its origin is from Ukraine and Moldova. It is usually made over the weekend with several family members participating in the cooking. It is a fun project with a tasty result!

A toast
To Being Rich!

Philosopher Diogenes said: "He has the most who is most content with the least." Being rich and being wealthy are two different things. The only person who is really rich is the one who is content with his life. Let's drink to
being rich!

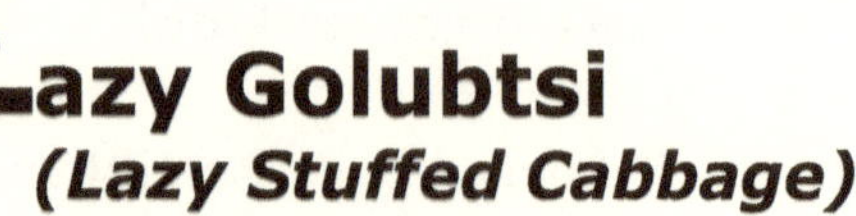

Lazy Golubtsi
(Lazy Stuffed Cabbage)

1 small head green cabbage
1 medium size onion
2 Tbsp olive oil
1 lb ground beef
3 Tbsp shopped tomatoes or 1 Tbsp tomato paste
½ lb cooked rice
2 Tbsp fresh parsley
Salt and pepper

Shred the cabbage, salt it and set aside. In a medium size saucepan sauté chopped onions in olive oil until translucent. Add the ground meat, tomatoes or tomato paste, salt and pepper and cook for 5 minutes. Add cabbage, a splash of water and cook for 10 minutes until the cabbage is cooked through. Add rice, mix and cook for 3 minutes more. Remove from heat and add parsley. Adjust seasoning. Serve with sour cream.

Makes 6 servings

This dish has the same ingredients as regular Golubtsi but does not require rolling the stuffing into the cabbage leaves. It is delicious!

A toast
When You Run Out of Toasts, Use This One

Let's hope that this is not the last one!

Potatoes with Mushrooms

4 large potatoes
6 Tbsp olive oil
1 package 14 oz baby portabella mushrooms
½ medium size onion
2 Tbsp fresh dill
Salt and pepper

Scrub potatoes and cut into French fry strips. Heat a large skillet on high, add 3 tablespoons of olive oil and potatoes. Reduce the heat to medium, salt the potatoes, cover and cook for 15-20 minutes stirring frequently until tender. Add olive oil if necessary.

In a separate medium size skillet sauté thinly sliced onions until translucent. Clean and thinly slice mushrooms. Add to the onions and cook on medium heat for 10-15 minutes until done and no liquid is left in the skillet. Season with salt and pepper. Add the mushroom mixture to the potatoes and mix. Cook for a couple of minutes for the flavors to mix. Add dill and adjust seasoning.

Makes 4 servings

This is a classic Russian dish – a combination of potatoes, mushrooms and dill. Highly recommended! Our guests devour these potatoes! This dish can be served as a main course or as a side dish.

Rack of Lamb
with Mustard Sauce

1 rack of lamb
2 Tbsp spicy Russian mustard (see separate recipe)
Salt and pepper

Trim fat from the rack, cut into individual ribs. Season the ribs with salt and pepper. Put ¼ teaspoon of mustard on each side of the rib meat and spread thinly to cover. Preheat the grill until hot. Grill lamb for about 10 minutes on each side.

Makes 2 servings

The mustard makes a savory crust on the surface of the meat ensuring that the lamb remains tender while it cooks. A simple but an absolutely fantastic dish!

A toast
A Perfect Match

In a popular Soviet movie in the 60s one of the characters lamented: "I have an opportunity to buy a goat but I am not interested. On the other hand, I wish to buy a horse but I cannot."

We often have an opportunity to get something that we are not interested in and wish to have something that we cannot get. Let's drink so that our wishes match our abilities.

Poached Salmon
with Dill Sauce

4 6 oz salmon fillets
2 Tbsp olive oil
1 8 oz bottle clam juice
¼ cup white wine
4 peppercorns
3 Tbsp chopped fresh dill
1 Tbsp lemon juice
1 cup sour cream or crème fraiche
Salt and pepper

Sprinkle salt on the salmon fillets. Coat each fillet with olive oil and sprinkle with lemon juice. Pour clam juice and wine into a medium size deep skillet, add peppercorns and salmon. Simmer for 5-7 minutes until salmon is opaque throughout.

For the sauce combine the sour cream, lemon juice and fresh dill. Season with salt. Stir gently. Serve salmon garnished with thin lemon slices, the sauce and fresh dill.

Makes 4 servings

Many Russian fish dishes call for poached or steamed fish, rarely fried. Sauces are served on the side. Fresh fish, even previously frozen, used to be hard to find in the times of the USSR. As a result, many Russians including my dad became avid fishermen. My dad was often successful and we had wonderful fish dinners. The combination of flavors in this dish is a classic Russian combination – fish, dill and sour cream.

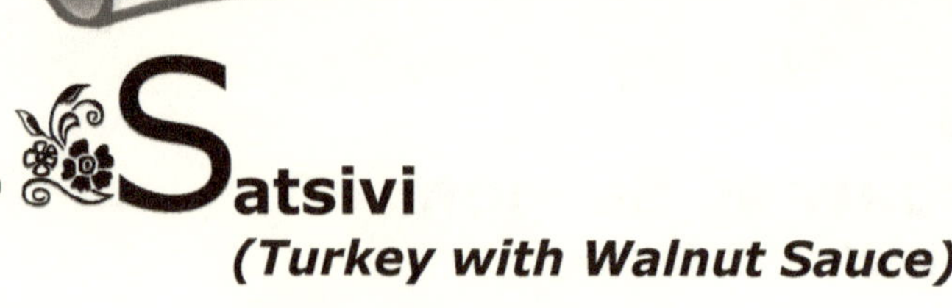

Satsivi
(Turkey with Walnut Sauce)

1 small turkey (6-8 lb)
2 quarts water
1 medium size onion
1 carrot
1 bay leaf
3 cups walnuts
2 eggs
2 cloves of garlic
2 Tbsp fresh cilantro, chopped
1 Tbsp fresh basil, chopped
¼ tsp curry powder
1 lemon
Salt and pepper

Cut turkey in pieces, cover with water in a large pot and bring to a boil. Skim the top and add onion, bay leaf, chopped carrots, salt and pepper. Cook for about 1 hour on low heat.

Chop walnuts in the food processor to a fine paste. Pour the chopped walnuts into about one quart of boiling broth. The sauce has to be thick, so start with less stock and add more if needed. Add garlic pressed through the garlic press to the broth, together with spices. Turn off the heat, cool for 30 minutes or so. Beat eggs in a small bowl. Slowly add the beaten eggs to the walnut mixture while it is still hot mixing continuously with a spoon. Add the juice from a half a lemon. Cut the turkey into bite size pieces and add to the walnut sauce. Adjust the seasoning and cool.

Makes 6-8 servings

Walnuts are one of the main components of Georgian cuisine. They were brought to the area in the 7th to 5th centuries BC. Walnut trees grow everywhere in Georgia even in the higher elevation areas of 5,000 ft. Walnuts are used in many vegetable dishes and sauces, soups, bean stews, meat and fish dishes as well as baking. The walnut sauce is a well known Georgian dish that can be made with turkey or chicken as well as fish. Unusual and delicious!

A toast
To Our Riches

A wealthy merchant met a prominent scientist on an international sea trip. The merchant was bringing many goods with him on the ship while the scientist did not have anything with him. The ship got into a terrible storm and sank. All passengers perished except the merchant and the scientist. Both found the same large wooden beam and held on tightly. After having been thrown around in the stormy ocean for awhile they found themselves on a deserted shore.

The merchant looked at the scientist and saw that he was extremely frightened and sad. He asked the scientist then: "Why are you so sad? It's me who should be sad, I lost all of my possessions but yours are all with you."

Let's raise a glass to the riches that we can never lose that are inside of us - our common sense, knowledge and wisdom!

Meat Stew
with Mushrooms

1 ½ lb beef
5 Tbsp olive oil
½ lb baby portabella mushrooms
4 potatoes
2 cups beef stock
1 Tbsp tomato paste
1 carrot
5 medium size onions
3 cloves of garlic
2 Tbsp finely chopped fresh dill
1 bay leaf
Salt and pepper

Cut meat against the grain into bite size strips. In a large skillet heat olive oil and brown the meat on both sides. Transfer into a medium size saucepan. Chop the onions. Add more oil to the skillet and sauté onions for 3 minutes. Add diced carrots and cook for another 3 minutes on medium heat. Transfer the mixture into the saucepan. Add beef stock, diced potatoes, the bay leaf and cook until potatoes are ready, about 10 minutes.

Clean and thinly slice mushrooms. Add more oil to the skillet and cook the mushrooms on medium heat until all liquid evaporates. Season with salt and pepper and transfer mushrooms to the saucepan. Add tomato paste, cook for a couple of minutes. Turn off the heat, add garlic pressed through the garlic press and dill. Adjust seasoning. Garnish with fresh dill if desired.

Makes 6 servings

A heartwarming dish for a family dinner in the winter time. Savory and filling! A classic Russian combination of ingredients – meat, mushrooms, potatoes and dill. Beef can be easily substituted by pork or chicken.

A tradition
Bread and Salt Tradition

"For you, dear guests, bread and salt," – this is how Russians welcome highly valued guests and newlyweds. The customary tradition of the bread and salt offering is also used on special occasions to bring luck. The guest is supposed to break off a piece of the offered bread, dip it in salt and eat it.

The custom is an expression of the proverbial Russian generosity and hospitality. According to a Russians proverb "Bread and salt conquer even the robbers," and Russians really believe it. Even the enemy, when defeated, found shelter and food in Russian homes. The word 'khlebosolny' means a hospitable person. It is derived from khleb, bread, and sol, salt. True to themselves, Russians would lavishly serve whatever they have in the kitchen and in the cellar to guests, travelers and foreigners who happen to visit their home.

Russians are bread lovers. There are over 200 varieties of breads in the country. Every Russian, on average, consumes over 110 pounds or 50 kilograms of bread annually. It is impossible to imagine a Russian table without bread. Russians treat bread with reverence. War veterans like my Mom can never throw bread away and would yell at anyone who attempts to do so, no matter how stale it may get!

Creamy Vegetarian Ragu
with Spaghetti Squash

1 small spaghetti squash
2 Tbsp sweet unsalted butter
½ medium size onion
2 Tbsp olive oil
1 carrot
½ eggplant
1 small zucchini
1 red bell pepper
1 tomato
¼ cup white wine
½ cup half and half or heavy cream
1 garlic clove
2 Tbsp fresh parsley
Salt and pepper

Cut the spaghetti squash in half and clean out the seeds. Put the halves face down into a low wide microwavable dish. Cover and cook in the microwave until tender, about 10 minutes.

In a large skillet heat the olive oil, add chopped onions and diced carrots and sauté until onions are translucent. Dice the eggplant, zucchini, pepper and tomato and add to the skillet. Add the wine, cover and cook for 5-7 minutes until the vegetables are tender, stirring occasionally. Add the cream and cook for another 1-2 minutes. Add garlic pressed through the garlic press and finely chopped parsley. Season with salt and pepper. Transfer into a serving bowl.

Using a fork, fluff the fibers of the spaghetti squash and scoop the insides into a serving bowl. Add butter and mix.

A tradition
The Tea (Chay) Ceremony

In Russia, tea is a major part of life. It is also an expression of hospitality. When you visit a Russian home during the day this is the drink you will be served with an assortment of sweet baked goods, fruit preserves, and sugar cubes. The belief is that after 20 minutes tea is not fresh. It has to be brewed and consumed right away.

Traditionally tea was served in very thin tall glasses placed in elaborate silver glass holders. It was served this way on long distance trains, such as Trans-Siberian railway. In homes, tea is served in wide cups with deep saucers. It is common to pour the piping hot tea into the saucer and drink it through a sugar cube held between your teeth. As the sugar melts in your mouth it sweetens the tea, sip by sip. Or you can do the same with fruit preserves. Eaten out of tiny bowls with a spoon the preserves also flavor your tea as they melt in your mouth with each sip.

It is believed that tea was first brought to Moscow by one of the Mongol khans in 1638. It was then imported from China and it is now grown in Georgia, Azerbaijan and other regions of Russia.

Tea is considered to be a drink that gives strength and is heartily recommended by Russians for many ailments.

Fish Cutlets

1 lb filet of fish
1 small onion
1 egg
3 Tbsp flour
1 Tbsp mayonnaise
2 Tbsp olive oil
Salt and pepper

Coarsely chop fish in the food processor. Non fatty fish is best. Transfer to a mixing bowl. Finely chop onions. Transfer to the bowl. Add the egg, mayonnaise, salt and pepper. Mix well. Add one tablespoon of flour at a time until the mixture reaches a sour cream consistency. Heat a medium size skillet and add olive oil. Drop one tablespoon of fish mixture on the skillet and brown on both sides, approximately 3 minutes per side on medium heat. Serve with sour cream or horseradish sauce. Garnish with dill or parsley if desired.

Makes 2 servings

This dish goes well with any potato side dish, especially the Yummy Potatoes. A cucumber salad is a great accompaniment creating a light and delicious meal.

Variations

It is common in Russia to add bread soaked in milk to all cutlet preparations. For this recipe 2 slices of bread soaked in a half cup of milk would be sufficient. Add the bread to the food processor after chopping the onions but before adding the mixture to the chopped fish. Russian cooks believe that the addition of bread makes the cutlets softer and yummier.

Leg of Lamb with Garlic

1 boneless leg of lamb butter-flied
1 head of garlic
Salt and pepper

Remove bones from a leg of lamb, remove extra fat and butterfly the meat. Butter a large cast iron pot and place the leg of lamb 'skin' down in the pot. Cut garlic into slivers. Pierce the meat with a small sharp knife and place garlic slivers into the openings ¾ inch apart from each other. Salt and pepper well.

Roast the leg of lamb at 425°F for 1 hour basting occasionally with released juices. Decrease the temperature to 400°F and cook for another 30 minutes. The resulting meat should be tender and juicy and there will be little liquid if at all left in the pot.

Makes 6 servings

This is easy to make and an absolutely delightful dish. It comes from Georgia where lamb is abundant and cooked in a multitude of ways. Serve with roasted vegetables and a Tomato and Onion or a Tomato with Onion and Arugula salad (see separate recipes).

⚞Dolma
(Stuffed Peppers and Other Vegetables)

1 lb ground beef
½ lb ground pork
1 egg
½ lb cooked rice
2 Tbsp finely chopped fresh parsley
2 medium size onions
3 cloves garlic
4 large red bell peppers
1 16 oz can stewed tomatoes
1 medium size tomato
4 Tbsp olive oil
½ cup heavy cream
1 tsp mixed herbs
1 cup shredded cheddar cheese
Salt and pepper

Preheat the oven to 350°. Cut red peppers in half lengthwise. Using a sharp knife make an incision at the base of the core, then remove the core with the seeds. Put peppers into a microwavable dish, cover and microwave on high for 5 minutes or so until almost cooked. Remove from microwave and let cool.

Finely chop onion and garlic in the food processor. Transfer to a mixing bowl. Add the first 5 ingredients, salt and pepper and mix well. Adding a couple of tablespoons of water if necessary, to reach desired consistency. The mixture should naturally and easily make a ball. Stuff pepper halves with the meat mixture, dividing equally and mounding slightly.

Coarsely chop tomatoes in the food processor, add cream, herbs, salt and pepper to taste. Pour over the peppers. Bake peppers for 25-30 minutes. When the stuffing reaches 165°F, the peppers are ready. Spread cheese over the peppers and broil in the oven for 5-10 minutes until golden brown. Serve with the tomato cream sauce and the sour cream. Garnish with chopped parsley if desired.

Makes 4 servings

Stuffed vegetables (Dolma) were introduced to Russia by Turks and became popular nationwide Russia. Any vegetable or fruit that can be hollowed out or wrapped around a filling can be used for dolma. The best stuffed dishes are still served in the Caucasus.

Stuffed Peppers is a classic Moldavian dish. It was not easy to buy good sweet peppers in the times of the Soviet Union. My dad worked hard to grow them himself from seeds in the St. Petersburg area. When we did not have peppers our family used zucchini and squash as stuffing vessels.

Variations

This dish can be varied in a number of ways:
- Use vegetarian stuffing instead of meat. The vegetarian stuffing can be made with carrots, onion, eggplant and zucchini, diced and cooked in olive oil with a little bit of tomato paste. Add garlic and dill at the end.
- Use feta instead of cheddar cheese. Moldavians prefer feta cheese in this dish.
- Add zucchini to the meat mixture and skip the rice to make it lighter.

# Chanahi
(Lamb in Crocks)

1 lb lamb
3 medium size potatoes
2 large tomatoes
½ large eggplant
½ lb green beans
2 medium size onions
4 cloves of garlic
2 tsp ground coriander
Salt and pepper

Prepare 4 personal size crocks. Each crock will make one serving. Cut lamb into small pieces and add to the crocks, 4-6 pieces into each. Chop the onions, add to the crocks. Peel and cut potatoes into ¼ inch rounds and add to the crocks. Cut tomatoes into quarters and add to the crocks. Trim and cut green beans into one inch pieces and divide between the crocks. Cut eggplant into quarters lengthwise and then into ¼ thick inch rounds. Add to the crocks. Add coriander, chopped garlic, salt and pepper. Pour 2 cups of water into each crock, cover and put into a 350° preheated oven. Cook for an hour and a half to two hours.

Makes 4 servings

This is another dish from Georgia that combines many local flavors that became widespread in Russia. This is a perfect dish for a family Saturday dinner. Not much cooking required since putting ingredients into the crocks takes about 15 minutes. And it smells SO great while the flavors slowly combine while the crocks sit in the oven!

Filet Mignon
with Mushroom Cream Sauce

4 1 ¾ thick filet mignon
1 medium size onion
1 8 oz package baby portabella mushrooms
½ cup heavy cream
2 Tbsp Madeira
2 Tbsp finely chopped fresh parsley
Salt and pepper

Heat the grill until hot. Spray the filets with olive oil and season with salt and pepper. Grill filet mignon for about 10 minutes on each side to be medium rare. In the meantime prepare the sauce. Chop onions and sauté in olive oil until translucent. Clean and thinly slice mushrooms and add them to the onions. Season with salt and pepper and cook until the liquid evaporates, about 10 minutes. Add Madeira, bring to a boil and then add cream. Cook for a minute or two until the cream thickens slightly. Serve immediately. Sauce can be spread on the plate under the steaks, served on the side or poured over the steaks.

Makes 4 servings

Our family loves this dish! It is simple but out of this world! We serve it when we get together to celebrate the end of a tough week or just to cheer us up. Serve with a glass of good Pinot Noir as has been the tradition in our family

Creamy Chicken
with Mushroom Sauce

2 lbs boneless and skinless chicken thighs
4 Tbsp olive oil
½ medium size onion
1 8 oz package white mushrooms
1 bay leaf
½ cup white wine
1 cup half and half or heavy cream
2 Tbsp fresh parsley
Salt and pepper

Cut chicken into bite size strips and brown on all sides in a skillet with olive oil. Transfer to a medium size saucepan, add wine and cook on low heat for 20 minutes. Add more oil to the skillet and cook chopped onion on low heat until translucent. Add sliced mushroom, salt and pepper and cook for 10-15 minutes stirring frequently until there is no liquid left in the skillet. Add the mushroom mixture to the chicken. Add cream. Bring to a boil and cook until the cream thickens slightly. Add parsley. Adjust seasoning. Serve over steamed broccoli or green beams.

Makes 4 servings

This dish has a classic Russian combination of chicken, mushrooms and cream. It is a savory dish that can be made quickly on a weekday night for a delicious and healthy dinner.

Eggplant Slices
with Garlic and Cheese

1 large eggplant
4 cloves of garlic
3 Tbsp mayonnaise
1 cup cheddar cheese

Cut the eggplant into ¼ inch slices lengthwise. In a cup combine the mayonnaise and garlic pressed through a garlic press. Prepare a baking sheet covered with foil. Spray with olive oil. Lightly salt the eggplant slices if desired. Arrange the slices on the baking sheet. Spread the mayonnaise mixture over the slices dividing equally. Spread cheese evenly over the slices. Cook in a 350° oven for 20 minutes or so until golden brown.

Makes 4 servings

This dish is simple to make, healthy and delectable! If you love garlic and eggplant, this is the dish for you!

A toast
To Harmony

If a man is persistent he will definitely achieve what his woman wants. Let's drink to a perfect match between the interests of men and the desires of women. To a strong and harmonious union of two hearts!

Liver Pate Torte

2 lbs beef liver
4 eggs
1 cup milk
4 large carrots, diced
4 medium size onions, chopped
4 Tbsp mayonnaise
2 Tbsp fresh parsley
Salt and pepper

Wash the liver and submerge into warm water for 5 minutes. Remove from the water and pat dry with paper towels. Remove membranes. Chop the liver in the food processor. Transfer into a mixing bowl and add beaten eggs and milk. Add salt and pepper and mix well.

Heat a small skillet 8 inches in diameter. Add olive oil. Pour about one fourth of the mixture on the skillet making sure to spread it evenly across the bottom. Cook for 2-3 minutes. Using two spatulas turn the whole liver pancake over and cook for another 2-3 minutes. Make four of such liver pancakes and set aside.

Cook onions and carrots in olive oil until ready. On a baking sheet place one liver pancake, spread a thin layer of mayonnaise on top and cover with a third of the carrot mixture. Put the second liver pancake on top. Repeat the process twice. Spread mayonnaise on the top liver surface and on the sides of the torte.

Preheat oven to 350°. Put the torte in the middle of the oven and cook for 15 minute. Before serving sprinkle the top with green onions and dill.

Makes 8 servings

This is an extravagant way to serve beef liver – a delight for liver lovers!

Variations

Instead of onions and carrots, use hard boiled eggs mixed with green onions. This will add an extra color to the already interesting presentation.

A toast
Peoples' Gossip

At the burial of her husband a young and beautiful widow publicly announced that she would never forget him nor marry again.

Three months passed and the widow seemed to have forgotten her statement. "And how are you going to deal with the peoples' gossip," – asked her relatives. "I am going to show you what peoples' gossip is really worth," – she said.

She took a little bell and tied it to the neck of a peacock and let him out on the street. People saw the peacock with a bell on his neck and started talking about him laughing. But in three days, everyone forgot about the peacock. "This is what is going to happen to me. They will talk about me for three days and then forget," – explained the widow to her relatives. Let's drink to people's gossip never disturbing us!

 Meat Cutlets

½ lb ground beef
½ lb ground pork
1 egg
½ medium size onion
2 cloves of garlic
½ cup water or milk
½ cup flour
4 Tbsp olive oil
Salt and pepper

Chop onions and garlic in a food processor. In a large mixing bowl mix ground beef and ground pork with salt, pepper, the onion mixture and the egg. Add water or milk in batches and mix well.

Put some flour on a large plate. Form cutlets and roll them in the flour. Heat a medium size skillet, add olive oil and fry cutlets on both sides on medium heat until golden brown. Test the readiness by prickling the top of a cutlet with a knife. If the juice that comes out is clear, the cutlet is ready.

Makes 6 cutlets

I remember coming home from school, opening the refrigerator and eating one of these cutlets cold. They are tasty and filling. They can be served with many sauces and side dishes. This is an extremely popular dish in Russian families.

Cabbage with Sausage

Peel and thinly slice the onion. Sauté with olive oil until translucent. Thinly slice the cabbage and add salt. Knead lightly with your hands so that the cabbage releases its juices. Add cabbage to the onions, cover and cook until tender on medium heat. If necessary, add a splash of water. Add chopped tomatoes and cook 5 minutes longer.

Cut the sausage into ¼ inch slices and fry in olive oil until golden. Add to the cabbage mixture. Remove from heat and add parsley.

Makes 6 servings

This dish was brought to Russia from Germany in the eighteenth century. However, sausages and hot dogs were not readily available during the Soviet era. As a result, this dish was somewhat of a delicacy even though it's hard to imagine it now.

Potato Cutlets
with Mushroom Sauce

4 large or 7 medium size potatoes
½ cup half and half
4 Tbsp sweet unsalted butter
1 egg
¾ cup flour
4 Tbsp olive oil
1 small onion
1 14 oz package baby portabella mushrooms
1 cup heavy cream
2 Tbsp each, fresh parsley and dill
Salt and pepper

Boil potatoes in their skins until done. Cool, peel and mash. Add butter, the egg, half and half, salt and pepper. Mix well to a consistency that can be molded into cutlets. Prepare a plate with flour. Drop a tablespoon of mixture into the flour forming a cutlet and coating it with flour on all sides. Heat a large skillet with olive oil. Brown cutlets on both sides, 3-4 minutes per side.

In a separate medium size skillet heat olive oil and sauté chopped onions until translucent. Add thinly sliced mushrooms, salt and pepper and cook until all water has evaporated. Add cream and bring to a boil. Cook for a couple of minutes until the cream thickens slightly. Add herbs and adjust seasoning.

Makes 4 servings

This is yet another combination of potatoes and mushrooms creating a lovely vegetarian dish that is popular in Russia. Serve it with Cucumber and Radishes salad (see separate recipe).

Chicken Rolls with Prunes

4 chicken breasts
4 pieces of bacon cut into halves
½ cup prunes
Salt and pepper

Pound the chicken breasts into thin cutlets between sheets of plastic wrap. Salt and pepper the chicken. Cut into 2 inch squares. Add a prune on top of each piece, roll and wrap with a piece of bacon. Secure the roll with a toothpick. Bake on a baking sheet at 350° for 20-25 minutes.

Makes 4 servings

You can use fish such as trout instead of chicken in this recipe. Comes out delicious! Prunes add an unusual sweetness contrasted by the saltiness of bacon. Enjoy!

A toast
Be Yourself

Once upon a time a donkey decided to become a lion. He wrapped himself in a lion's skin and walked around pretending to be a lion. From a distance other animals could not distinguish him from a real lion and feared him. He even made a herd of cows flee. But when a gust of wind ripped the lion's skin off the donkey, the angry animals beat him up. Let's drink to us being ourselves and not pretending to be either lions or donkeys.

Oladushki
(Pancakes)

2 cups kefir or buttermilk
2 eggs
1 tsp sugar
Pinch of salt
1 tsp baking powder
10-12 Tbsp flour
Olive oil
Unsalted butter
Salt and pepper

In a mixing bowl beat the eggs, add salt, sugar and one cup of kefir. Add baking powder and mix well. Add flour to this mixture in batches mixing well. Add the remaining kefir. The batter should be at sour cream consistency.

Heat a skillet on high heat until really hot. Add olive oil. Reduce heat to medium. Drop one tablespoon of batter on the skillet to form a pancake. Cook for 2 minutes or so per side. Transfer to a plate and spread butter on top. Repeat with the rest of the batter. Serve with butter, sour cream and your favorite jam.

Makes 4 servings

Pancakes are considered to be a breakfast food in the US. Not so in Russia. You can find them served for lunch as well as for dinner with various accompaniments such as cottage cheese, jams and meat.

Zucchini Pancakes

1 medium size zucchini
1 egg
½ tsp salt
2-3 Tbsp flour
Olive oil
Sour cream

Cut zucchini into rounds and coarsely chop in a food processor. Transfer into a mixing bowl, add salt, the egg and mix. Add flour and mix well.

Heat a skillet until really hot. Add olive oil. Reduce heat to medium. Drop one tablespoon of batter on the skillet to form a pancake. Cook 3-4 minutes on each side. Cover if necessary. Transfer to a plate. Serve with sour cream and milk.

Makes 2 servings

You can use chopped carrots instead of zucchini in this recipe. We make these pancakes for lunch often. They are light and yummy!

A toast
The Russian Way...

In England, the rule is that you can do anything except what is forbidden. In Germany, you cannot do anything except what is allowed. In France, everything is allowed even things that are forbidden. In Russia, you cannot do anything even things that are allowed. Let's drink to rules that are made to be broken!

Dranniki
(Potato Pancakes)

6 potatoes
1 egg
2 Tbsp flour
Salt and pepper
Olive oil
Sour cream

Peel potatoes and shred in a medium shredder. Add the egg, flour, salt and pepper and mix well.

Heat a skillet until really hot. Add olive oil. Reduce heat to medium. Drop one tablespoon of potatoes on the skillet to form a drannik. Cook 3-4 minutes on each side until golden brown. Cover if necessary. Transfer to a plate. Serve with sour cream.

Makes 4 servings

This dish came to Russia from the Baltic republics, Estonia and Latvia. The scrumptious potato delights can be served as a side dish with fish or chicken. They can also be served as a main dish. They go well with the Cucumber, Radish and Dill salad (see separate recipe).

Sirniki
(Farmer's Cheese Cakes)

½ lb farmer's cheese
1 egg
1 Tbsp sugar
Pinch of salt
½ cup flour
Olive oil
Sour cream

In a mixing bowl mix the farmer's cheese, egg, sugar and salt. Put a little bit of flour on a large plate. Drop one tablespoon of cheese mixture into the flour. Roll in flour on all sides forming a cake.

Heat a skillet until really hot. Add olive oil. Reduce heat to medium. Cook 3-4 minutes on each side until golden brown. Cover the skillet if necessary. Transfer to a plate. Serve with sour cream and milk.

Makes 4 servings

Farmer's cheese is a staple of Russian cuisine. It is almost never sold salted. Its taste differs from the varieties of farmer's cheese sold in the US. This dish came to Russia from the Baltic republics, Estonia and Latvia. It is often served for lunch. Ricotta cheese can be used instead of farmer's cheese in this recipe.

Beliashi
(Open Meat Pies)

2 containers Pillsbury buttermilk biscuits
1 lb ground lamb
1 lb ground pork
1 lb ground beef
1 large onion
2 cups water
Salt and pepper
Olive oil

Sprinkle flour on a clean surface. Open the containers of biscuits, separate the biscuits, put them on the flour, cover with a clean towel and let stand for 10 minutes or so.

Finely chop the onion in the food processor. In a large bowl combine the meats, onion, salt and pepper and water. Knead well with your hands.

Roll each biscuit with a rolling pin until thin. Place a tablespoon of the meat mixture in the middle of each biscuit. Make a triangle shape pinching the dough together and leaving a small hole in the middle of each pie.

Heat a medium size skillet with olive oil covering the bottom. Fry beliashi on each side, starting with the side with the opening, 4-5 minutes per side.

Makes 4 servings

A couple of members of our family will drive long distances to eat these delicious concoctions. They are absolutely tremendous on a cold day and have to be eaten with vodka. Some people can eat as many as 10!

Sashlik
(Summer Kebabs)

2 ½ lbs pork or lamb
4 large onions
1 cup balsamic vinegar
½ cup red wine
3 Tbsp olive oil
3 Tbsp fresh parsley
3 Tbsp fresh cilantro
6 plum tomatoes
3 bell peppers, red, green and yellow
Salt and pepper

Cut the meat into bite-size pieces. Finely chop one onion. Combine meat, chopped onions, chopped herbs with salt and pepper. Cut the other onions into ¼ inch rounds. In a separate bowl alternate a layer of meat with a layer of onion rounds. In a small bowl combine the vinegar, red wine, olive oil, salt and pepper. Pour the marinade on top of the meat and onions. Press the meat down, cover with a plate and put a weight on top. Marinate for 3-4 hours.

Thread cubes of meat on separate skewers alternating with onions, tomatoes and peppers. Grill for 3-5 minutes per side.

Makes 6 servings

Sashlik is an Armenian every day pleasure. The dish is now common across Russia. Traditionally, the preparation and cooking of shashlik is entirely in the hands of men. .Men compete in creating different marinades to make their shashlik tastier and more tender.

Sides and Salads

Sides and salads are served together with the main course. It is customary to serve sides and salads on big platters and in bowls that are put in the middle of the table so that guests can help themselves. This section contains green salads that are the recent additions to the Russian menu and many classic tasty sides that can be fantastic meals by themselves.

Sides and Salads

Caesar Salad

½ head Romaine lettuce
2 garlic cloves
1 tsp mustard
1 Tbsp balsamic vinegar
1 tsp lemon juice
1 Tbsp Worcestershire sauce
1 Tbsp water
4-6 Tbsp olive oil
Salt and pepper
1 cup shredded Parmesan cheese

Wash the lettuce, shake off the water or pat dry with the paper towels. Cut into desired pieces for salad.

For the dressing, press garlic through the garlic press into a small bowl or a glass. Add mustard, Worcestershire sauce and vinegar and mix well. Add water. Using a small whisk or a fork gradually whisk olive oil into the mixture. Season with salt and pepper and add lemon juice to taste. Before serving, add the dressing to the greens together with the Parmesan cheese and mix well.

Makes 4 servings

For some reason Romaine salad was not grown in Russia. In fact in the times of the Soviet Union, green lettuces were in short supply. As a result, visitors to Russia did not see that many green salads on the menu.

I am sure that every family develops their favorite variation of the Caesar salad by adjusting the dressing. Our family loves garlic and likes light dressings. This is our favorite way of serving the Caesar salad.

Rice with Onions

Combine rice with 2 and ¼ cups of water, 1 Tbsp olive oil, salt and pepper and cook on low heat until all liquid has evaporated.

In parallel, sauté onion in a skillet with olive oil until translucent. When the rice is ready, add butter and the sautéed onions and mix well. Adjust seasoning and serve.

Makes 4 servings

This is a classic Russian side dish that goes well with many main courses. It goes particularly well with Chicken Kiev, Chicken cutlets, fish and seafood dishes.

A toast
Who is Wise and Who is Stupid?

A philosopher was asked: "Who is wise and who is stupid?" "It is really very simple," – replied the philosopher. "The one who reaches his goal is wise and the one who does not is stupid." Let's drink to each of us reaching our most cherished goals!

Cucumber and Dill Salad

4 pickling cucumbers
3 Tbsp fresh dill
1 Tbsp white vinegar
3 Tbsp olive oil
Salt

Slice cucumbers thinly, add the other ingredients and mix well.

Makes 4 servings

This is another classic Slavic dish. It goes well with any potato dish or side, such as fried potatoes with mushrooms and dill.

A toast
A Baby Test

There is an old tradition to put a book and a glass of wine in front of a new born baby. If the baby reaches for the book, the person will be a scientist and if for the wine – a party lover. But once upon a time a baby was born and his parents put a book and a glass with wine in front of him. He reached for both - the wine and the book! Let's drink to people who can combine a drive for knowledge with having a good time!

Spinach Salad
with Mushrooms and Bacon

1 lb fresh baby spinach
4 slices lean bacon
2 Tbsp onion
½ lb baby portabella mushrooms
2 Tbsp white vinegar
1 cup apple cider
1 Tbsp olive oil
Salt

Cut bacon into small pieces and cook in a large skillet over low heat, stirring frequently until it is crisp. Transfer to paper towels and retain the fat. Add vinegar, cider, salt and pepper to the skillet. Bring the mixture to a boil and boil it down until it is reduced to ½ cup. Whisk the oil and adjust the seasoning. In a large bowl toss the spinach with the warm dressing until it is just slightly wilted. Add thinly sliced onions and mushrooms and mix. Transfer to plates and sprinkle the salad with bacon.

Makes 4 servings

This is a delightful salad that combines the crispness of onions with the sweetness of the cider and the tartness of vinegar.

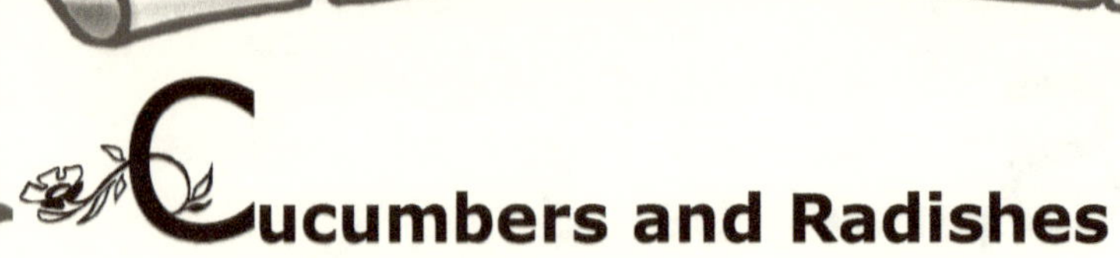 Cucumbers and Radishes

4 pickling cucumbers
1 bunch fresh radishes (sold with greens)
3 Tbsp fresh dill
2 Tbsp sour cream
Salt

Use young cucumbers for this dish. Pickling cucumbers are best. Make sure to cut off the skin at the stem side because it can be bitter. Thinly slice cucumbers and radishes. Toss them with salt in a medium size serving bowl and let stand for a couple of minutes. Add sour cream and dill. Mix well.

Makes 4 servings

This is a classic Slavic dish and is often served as a part of the zakuski table. Some families prefer shredding the radishes and cutting cucumbers into tiny thin slices. Try it both ways and enjoy!

A toast
To Great Friends!

In Russia there is a belief that time spent with friends is not counted in your age. Let's drink to friends who preserve our youth!

Tomato and Onion Salad

3 large ripe tomatoes (Ugly tomatoes are best)
¼ large onion
1 Tbsp white vinegar
3 Tbsp olive oil
Salt and pepper

Quarter tomatoes, cut each quarter crosswise into thin slices and put them into a large serving bowl. Make sure to put all the juices released in the process of cutting into the bowl. Slice the onion as thinly as possible and add to the tomatoes.

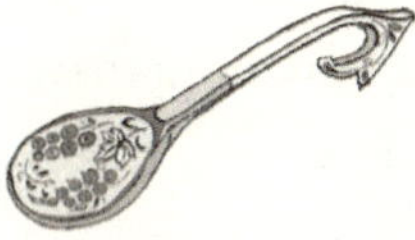

Before serving add salt and pepper, vinegar and oil to the tomatoes and mix well. Tomatoes will release lots of juice. Taste and adjust the seasoning.

Makes 4 servings

This is one of our favorite salads! Its roots are from Georgia and Uzbekistan where it is served mostly with lamb dishes. The sweetness of onions and the sourness of tomatoes make it a perfect combination with the richness of lamb.

Variations

Proceed as the above recipe and add young arugula leaves to the salad. The tartness of arugula goes extremely well with this tomatoes and onions combination.

Spinach Salad
with Grapefruit Dressing

1 lb fresh baby spinach
2 Tbsp onion
1 large grapefruit
4-5 baby portabella mushrooms
1 Tbsp balsamic vinegar
1 Tbsp olive oil
Salt and pepper

Peel the grapefruit, separate the grapefruit meat from the membranes and cut into bite size chunks. Slice onion and mushrooms thinly. In a medium size bowl toss spinach, mushrooms, onion with grapefruit sections and oil and vinegar. Season with salt and pepper.

Makes 4 servings

Grapefruit and spinach are great accompaniments to meats and promote digestion. This is a healthy salad that goes well with any meat dish.

A toast
People Are Strange

People are strange – they despair when they lose money but are fine with mindlessly living day after day losing them irreversibly. Let's drink to having our days filled with purpose!

Russian Coleslaw

½ medium size green cabbage
1 medium size carrot
1 large apple, such as Honey Crisp
3 Tbsp fresh parsley, chopped
3 Tbsp mayonnaise
1-2 tsp lemon juice
Salt and pepper to taste

Slice cabbage thinly or shred in the food processor. Add salt and knead as if you are kneading dough until cabbage releases some juice. Shred the carrot in a medium size shredder and add to cabbage. Peel and core the apple. Shred in the medium size shredder and add to cabbage. Add parsley and mayonnaise and mix well. If the apple is sweet, add lemon juice and adjust seasoning.

Makes 4 servings

Most families in Russia who have dachas grow and store cabbage for the winter. It has been a tradition for generations. As a result, cabbage is used in many dishes. This recipe is sometimes used as a part of the zakuski table but most often it is served as a salad with a chicken or fish main course.

Variations

There are many variations to this basic recipe.
- Add ¼ cup onion chopped finely.
- Add celery, red and green pepper for color and taste.

Yummy Potatoes

4 large potatoes
2 Tbsp unsalted sweet butter
¼ cup half and half or heavy cream
Salt and pepper to taste

Scrub potatoes clean and dice them unpeeled. Put into a microwavable dish, sprinkle with salt and pepper, add cubed butter and 2 tablespoons of half and half. Mix well. Microwave covered for 5 minutes. Take potatoes out of the microwave, mix, add some more half and half if needed and return to the microwave for another 2 minutes. Check whether potatoes are ready and if not, repeat the process – mix, add some more half and half and cook a little longer. Adjust seasoning.

Makes 4 servings

My grandmother used to cook potatoes that had been previously boiled unpeeled. She would peel and dice them and cook them with milk and butter in a skillet. These were my favorite potatoes because of how they got coated in the rich milk and butter sauce. Using the microwave, this dish resembles my grandmother's cooking except that it is much quicker and easier. In addition, these potatoes taste as baked, not boiled.

A superstition
Fending off Bad Luck

Russians say that you have forgotten something and must return home, you should look at yourself in the mirror. Returning is considered to be bad luck but looking in the mirror fends it off.

Braised Cabbage

1 medium size onion chopped
1 large carrot diced
2 Tbsp olive oil
2 cups shredded green or red cabbage
1 cup sauerkraut
1 cup chicken broth
½ cup white wine
1 bay leaf
Salt and pepper

Sauté onion with carrots in a large pot until the onion is translucent. Add cabbage, sauerkraut and chicken stock. The proportion of cabbage to sauerkraut controls the sourness of the dish. The most balanced dish comes out when the amount of cabbage and sauerkraut is similar by volume. This proportion is easier to see after the pot is brought to a simmer. After simmering, adjust the proportion and add wine, the bay leaf, salt and pepper. Cook on low heat until all liquid has evaporated. Add parsley, adjust the seasoning and serve. If the resulting dish comes out too sour, add a pinch of sugar or sugar substitute. If this is not served with a fatty main dish such is a roasted duck, add 2 Tbsp of butter.

Makes 4 servings

Russian cuisine is a mixture of peasant cooking influenced by European cuisine during and after the reign of Peter the Great in the 18th century. This recipe comes from Germany. This vegetarian side dish classically goes with the roasted duck or can be served by itself. It can be also served with sausages and cutlets.

Sweet Peppers with Dill

6 large bell peppers of different colors
3 Tbsp olive oil
2 Tbsp fresh dill
2 Tbsp white wine
Salt and pepper

Core and cut bell peppers into inch size squares. Heat a skillet; add olive oil, bell peppers, wine, salt and pepper. If using dry dill add it to the pepper mixture. Cook on low heat under cover for 5-6 minutes or until peppers are tender. If using fresh dill, add it at the end when peppers are ready to serve.

Makes 4 servings

This is a wonderful, easy to make side dish that goes well with many main dishes - any meat, fish or poultry. It can be also used as a stuffing for the boned turkey recipe.

A toast
May We Be Ashamed...

Two men are walking down the street talking. Suddenly one of them turns to the other: "Can I hide behind your back? I see our doctor walking towards us and I'd like to avoid talking to him." "What's the matter?" – asked the other. The first responded: "I am really ashamed! I have not been to see him in ten years!" Let's drink to our health and may we be ashamed of not seeing our doctors!

Roasted Sweet Potatoes
with Rosemary and Parmesan

2 lbs sweet potatoes
8 Tbsp olive oil
3 garlic cloves
3 medium red onions
½ cup Parmesan cheese
1 Tbsp fresh rosemary
Salt and pepper to taste

Set one rack in the center of the oven and one at the lowest position. Preheat oven to 375°. Line 2 baking sheets with foil. Peel potatoes and cut in strips. In a bowl toss them with salt, pepper, garlic pressed through the garlic press and six tablespoons of olive oil. Spread on one baking sheet in a single layer and place on the center rack.

Peel onions, halve each one and cut crosswise into thin 1/8 inch slices. In a bowl coat the onions with the remaining oil and salt and pepper. Spread on the second baking sheet in a single layer and place on the low rack.

Roast until potatoes and onions are tender, about 30 minutes stirring every 10 minutes or so. Combine potatoes and onions in a serving bowl, sprinkle with Parmesan cheese and rosemary. Adjust seasoning.

Makes 4 servings

A savory dish that can be served by itself or as an accompaniment to chicken, fish or meat.

Rice with Mushrooms

1 cup long grain rice
3 Tbsp olive oil
1 8 oz package white mushrooms
½ medium size onion sliced
2 Tbsp butter
Salt and pepper

Combine rice with 2 and ¼ cups of water, 1 Tbsp of olive oil, salt and pepper and cook on low heat until all liquid has evaporated.

In parallel, sauté onions with olive oil until translucent in a skillet. Add sliced mushrooms, salt and pepper and cook until the liquid has evaporated.

When the rice is ready, add cubed butter and the mushroom mixture and mix well. Adjust seasoning and serve.

Makes 4 servings

This is a classic Russian side dish that goes well with many main courses. It particularly goes well with Chicken Kiev, Chicken cutlets, fish and seafood dishes.

A superstition
Drink to It!

In Russia it is believed that if you raise your glass for a toast, you cannot put it down before drinking. If you do, this action cancels the toast and you have to start all over again.

Potato & Meat Casserole

2 lbs potatoes
1 egg
1 cup milk
2 lbs ground beef
2 medium size onions
3 Tbsp unsalted sweet butter
½ cup shredded cheddar cheese
Salt and pepper to taste

Peel potatoes, cut each into 3 to 5 pieces and boil in salted water until tender. Add butter, hot milk and slightly beaten egg. Mash the potatoes and then whisk to medium thickness adding milk if necessary. Adjust seasoning.

In a large skillet melt the butter and sauté chopped onions until translucent. Add ground meat and cook until done, stirring frequently. Season with salt and pepper. Add a pinch of cayenne if desired.

Prepare an oiled casserole dish. Put half of the potato mixture at the bottom, spread the meat mixture on the potato layer and then cover with the remaining potatoes. Sprinkle with olive oil and cheese. Bake at 350° for 30 minutes until golden on top.

Makes 6-8 servings

This is a classic Russian casserole that can be served as a separate meal with a salad or as a side dish.

Green Beans with Garlic

2 lbs green beans
3 Tbsp unsalted sweet butter
2 garlic cloves
Salt and pepper to taste

Trim green beans and cut into 1 inch pieces. Bring water to boil in a medium size pot, add salt and beans. Cook beans for 3 minutes until tender but crisp. Strain the beans and rinse in cold water to stop the cooking process. In a serving bowl toss beans with butter and garlic pressed through the garlic press. Serve immediately.

Makes 6-8 servings

In our family this simple combination became a staple side dish since we all love beans and garlic. It goes well with any chicken, fish or meat dish.

A toast
Between the First and the Second

Let's drink to the company and the food being so great that we always want to have another shot between the first and the second one!

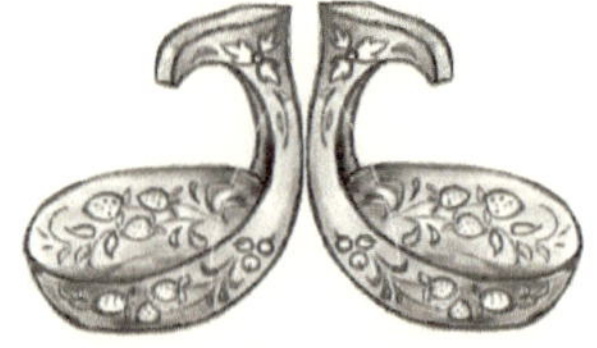

Mushroom Ragu

1 14 oz package white mushrooms
3 Tbsp olive oil
1 onion
2 Tbsp fresh parsley or dill
Salt and pepper

Heat a medium size skillet, add olive oil. Sauté chopped onions until translucent. Clean and slice mushrooms, add to the skillet, season with salt and pepper. Cook until done and no liquid is left in the skillet. Add finely chopped parsley or dill depending on how this ragu will be used. Adjust seasoning to taste.

Makes 4 servings

In Russia mushrooms are used in a variety of dishes. This is a basic preparation that can be then made into a sauce by adding cream and liquor. Or this ragu can be added to potatoes to make a wonderful potato and mushroom side dish. Or this ragu can be heaped on a steak adding flavor to the meal.

A superstition
Safe Journey

In Russia, when guests leave after a long stay, the hostess is not supposed to clean up after them, such as washing the dishes or laundry, until the guests arrive at their destination. Cleaning is considered to be bad luck for the journey.

Scalloped Potatoes

4 lbs Russet potatoes
4 Tbsp unsalted sweet butter
¼ cup finely chopped onion
3 cups whole milk
2 cups grated cheddar cheese
Salt and pepper to taste

Preheat oven to 400°. Lightly oil a glass baking dish - 13x9x2-inch is best. Peel and cut potatoes into ¼ inch thick rounds. Arrange in the baking dish overlapping slightly. Sprinkle with salt, pepper and onion. Put small pieces of butter across the top and sprinkle one cup of cheese. Top with remaining potatoes. Salt and add pepper to this layer.

Bring milk to a boil in a small saucepan or in the microwave. Pour milk over the potatoes. Cover the baking dish with foil and bake for 45 minutes. Uncover the dish and sprinkle potatoes with the remaining cheese. Bake uncovered for 30 minutes or so until the potatoes are tender and the cheese becomes golden. Let stand for 5-10 minutes before cutting and serving.

Makes 10-12 servings

Russian cuisine was greatly influenced by European cooking in the eighteen and nineteen century starting with the reign of Peter the Great. Russians are potato lovers and this French inspired dish became one of the favorites. This side dish is often served in the finest restaurants in Russia and is customary at family holiday tables.

Mashed Potatoes

1 lb potatoes
4 Tbsp unsalted sweet butter
1 cup whole milk
Salt and pepper to taste

Peel potatoes, cut each into 3 to 5 pieces and boil in salted water until tender. Strain the potatoes. Add butter and a quarter of the hot milk and start mashing. Add more milk and continue mashing until the desired consistency is reached. Adjust seasoning.

Makes 6-8 servings

There is nothing extraordinary about this recipe. It is included because it is a part of our family's menu. We love mashed potatoes! Many things can be added to make this basic recipe into a complex dish – onion, garlic, herbs, roasted peppers, asparagus, avocado, etc.

A superstition
Beware, Unmarried Women

In Russia unmarried women are encouraged to sit at the side of a table, never at the corner. It is believed that if they sit at the corner they will not get married.

Soups

Since many regions of Russia are cold in the winter, Russians love soups. Soups are usually served as a first course for 'obed' (late lunch, around 2pm) or as a meal for a light late dinner. This section presents many flavorful and satisfying soups that will be great additions to any menu.

Soups

Uha
(Russian Fish Soup)

A whole salmon, 7-9 lbs
3 large potatoes
8 black peppercorns
1 medium onion
1 leek
1 bay leaf
1 carrot
2 stalks celery
2 Tbsp parsley
1 can tomatoes
2 quarts water
Salt

Clean the fish, remove the head, separate bones from the flesh. Bring the bones and the fish head to boil in a large pot with water. Skim off the foam, add quartered onion, carrots, celery and leeks cut in large chunks. Salt and pepper and add the bay leaf. Continue to boil on low heat for 1.5 hours. Strain the soup.

Cut the tail end of the salmon into steaks, add to the strained liquid and continue to cook for 20-30minutes until the fish is done. Add potatoes cut into small cubes in 10-15 minutes. At the same time put one or two cups of stock into a small pot, add tomatoes and parsley and cook for 10 minutes or so. Strain and add to the soup when potatoes and fish are done.

Makes 8 servings

This soup is really delicious and can be the whole dinner if served with rye bread and butter. Do not forget a shot of vodka. It goes super well with this soup!

Russians love to spend time in nature fishing and hunting. I remember when my dad made this soup in a pot over a fire on a lake shore. When it is prepared using wild fish, it is called triple uha. The tiny, non edible fish is cooked first and then taken out of the pot. Bones and heads of larger fish are cooked next and then taken out. And only then the best chunks of fish meat are added together with vegetables if they are available. Every Russian fisherman carries a bay leaf and black peppercorns with them just in case they catch the right fish.

A toast
Judging Each Other

Armenian radio asks: "What would happen if an Armenian goes to court with a Jew?"

Answer: "The judge will get a 10 year sentence."

It's better, at least for the safety of the judges that neither Armenians nor Jews end up in court. Let's drink to that we are not judged and we do not judge.

The above toast refers to the fact that the Armenian and Jewish people in the former USSR were respected for their advanced ability for wise and compassionate discourse. Many Russian jokes start with 'Armenian (or Georgian, etc.) radio asks'.

Chicken Noodle

2 ½ quarts water
1 lb chicken parts with bones
1 large potato
4 black peppercorns
1 bay leaf
1 carrot
1 stalks celery
2 Tbsp fresh parsley
¾ cup dry noodles
Salt and pepper

Pour water into a medium pot, add chicken, the bay leaf, peppercorns, carrots and celery cut into small cubes, and bring to a boil. Reduce heat and skim off the foam. Add salt and cook for 30 minutes skimming the top occasionally. Add cubed potatoes and let the soup cook for another 10 minutes. Add noodles and cook for 5 minutes or so until the noodles are tender and the potatoes are cooked through. Turn off the heat, remove the chicken from the soup, add parsley and adjust seasoning. Take the chicken meat off the bones, cut the meat into small bites and return to the pot.

Makes 4 servings

This simple recipe makes a delicious and distinctive soup different from other chicken noodle soups that you have ever tried. When you taste it you will know that it is home made. Enjoy!

Split Pea Soup

2 ½ quarts water
2 smoked pork hocks ('ryulka' in Russian)
1 ½ cups green split peas
1 bay leaf
½ medium size onion
1 large carrot
1 large potato
2 Tbsp fresh parsley
Salt and pepper

Pour water into a medium pot. Add pork, bay leaf, carrots cut in small cubes, chopped onion and split peas. Bring to a boil and skim the top. Cook on low heat for 30 minutes. The peas will be well cooked through and some of them will be dissolving into the broth. Add cubed potatoes, salt and pepper and cook for another 15 minutes. When potatoes are done, turn off the heat, remove ryulka, add parsley and adjust the seasoning. The meat from the ryulka can be cut into small pieces and added back to the pot. Add cayenne pepper if desired. Serve with bread and butter.

Makes 4 servings

This is a delicious and hearty soup for a cold day. It is easy to make and great to have on hand in the refrigerator during the long, cold winter months.

Russians rarely add flour to thicken soups and, as a result, soups taste differently from their counterparts served in other parts of the world. If thicker consistency is desired, add more peas next time.

Chahohbili
(Chicken in Cilantro Broth)

1 medium size chicken (4-5 lb)
4 Tbsp olive oil
3 quarts water
1 bay leaf
3 medium size onions
3 large tomatoes
1 bunch of cilantro
3 garlic cloves
Salt and pepper

Cut chicken into serving size pieces and brown the skin side in a large skillet with olive oil. Transfer to a large pot, barely cover with water, and add salt, pepper and the bay leaf. Bring to a boil. Skim the top and cook for 30 to 45 minutes until chicken is tender. Chop onions, tomatoes and add to the boiling chicken. Cook for 10 minutes or so. Remove from heat. Add finely chopped cilantro and garlic pressed through the garlic press. Adjust seasoning. Serve with crusty white bread.

Makes 6 servings

This is a tremendous soup that is light and delicious! It comes from Georgia. If you like tomatoes, cilantro and garlic, this is the soup for you.

Mushroom Soup

Pour chicken stock into a medium pot. Add carrots cut into small cubes, cubed potatoes and bay leaf. Bring to a boil and skim the top. Cook on low heat for 10 minutes.

Clean and slice mushrooms thinly. Heat a medium size skillet. Add olive oil and sauté chopped onions until translucent. Add mushrooms, salt and pepper. Cook on medium heat until cooked but crisp. Add the mushroom mixture to the soup. Cook for another 5 minutes. If the vegetables are done, turn off the heat, add finely chopped dill and parsley. Adjust the seasoning. Serve with a spoonful of sour cream and dill sprinkled on top.

Makes 4 servings

A variety of mushrooms can be used in this soup or just simple white mushrooms. The broader variety of mushrooms used, the better the taste. Since Russians pick wild mushrooms, dry them and then reconstitute them, this soup usually has lots of flavor.

Borshch

3 quarts beef or lamb stock
1 lb cooked lamb or beef meat
½ head green cabbage
1 potato
1 large carrot
1 celery stalk
1 bay leaf
1 onion
2 Tbsp olive oil
2 large beets
1 tsp vinegar
1 large ripe tomato
1 red bell pepper
2 Tbsp dill
2 Tbsp fresh parsley
Sour cream
1 large garlic clove
Salt and pepper

Prepare beef or lamb stock separately. Combine the stock, thinly sliced cabbage, peeled and cubed potatoes, cubed carrots and the bay leaf in a large saucepan. Bring to a boil and continue to simmer on low heat.

Heat a large skillet. Add olive oil and sauté chopped onions until translucent. Peel and shred beets in a medium size shredder. Add to the skillet with vinegar and mix. Add chopped tomato and cubed red bell pepper, salt and pepper. Cover the skillet and cook until the beets are tender, about 10-15 minutes. Add oil if necessary. When ready, add the beet mixture to the pot with potatoes and cabbage and cook for 5 minutes to combine the flavors. Remove from heat. Add garlic pressed through the garlic press, parsley and dill.

Adjust seasoning. Serve with a dollop of sour cream and dill sprinkled on top.

Makes 8 servings

This is a classic Russian recipe of a famous borshch. The key to the recipe is the strength of the stock (less water, more bones and meat). In Ukraine it is also customary to add pork fat to the stock, which makes it even tastier. Or serve borsch with rye bread and thinly sliced cured pork fat just taken out of the freezer. This combination is hard to beat especially when served with a shot of cold vodka.

A toast
Gods' Pearls

Greek mythology has this story. It happened way before there was life on earth. There lived two gods of beauty and they had one pearl. This pearl was so beautiful that these gods had trouble having enough time to admire it in solitude. They settled the dispute by having it on display at one god's home one day and at the other's another day.

There came a day when the gods argued about this pearl. In anger they started pulling at it in two different directions. The pearl could not handle it and fell apart. The tiny particles fell on earth.

I am sure that these little pearl particles are sitting here with us. Let's drink to the beautiful pearls, our women!

Solyanka
(Soup with Pickles and Meat)

½ lb pork with a bone
¼ lb smoked pork
¼ lb smoked sausage
2 medium size onions
1 medium size carrot
2 potatoes
4 half sour pickles
3 Tbsp tomato paste
Lemon
2 Tbsp pitted black olives
2 Tbsp each fresh parsley and dill
Salt

Peel and finely chop one onion and cook until tender in a skillet with olive oil. Put pork with the bone, a whole peeled onion and the carrot in a large saucepan with water and bring to a boil. Skim the top, salt and cook on low heat until the meat is ready approximately 40 minutes. Take out the meat and the veggies.

Peel and cut potatoes into small cubes and cook in the stock until done, 10 minutes or so. Add diced pickles, tomato paste and sautéed onions and bring to a boil. Add cubed meat, cubed smoked pork and cubed sausage and cook on low heat for 5 minutes or so. Remove from heat. Adjust seasoning and add parsley and dill. Serve with a dollop of sour cream, add a thin slice of lemon and sprinkle thinly sliced olives and chopped herbs if desired.

Makes 4 servings

This is an unusual but tremendously satisfying soup for a cold day!

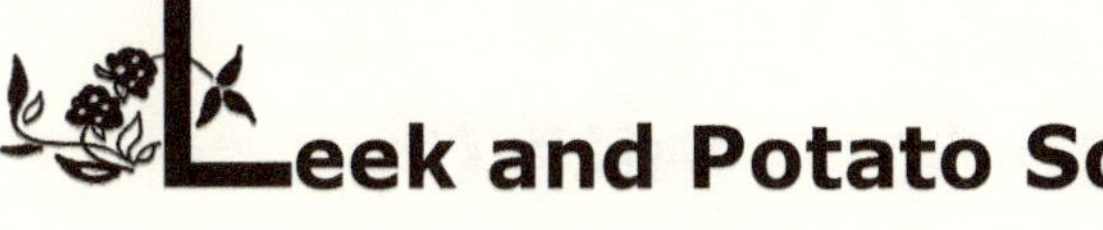eek and Potato Soup

4 Tbsp unsalted butter
6 leeks
4 cups chicken stock
2 large potatoes
A dash of nutmeg
1 ½ to 2 cups sour or heavy cream
Chopped chives
Salt and pepper

Clean leeks, slice the white and lightly green parts into ¼ inch slices. Melt butter in a skillet and cook the leeks gently, tossing them lightly, for a few minutes. Bring chicken stock to a boil. Peel and cube potatoes. Lower the heat, add potatoes and simmer until potatoes are tender. Add leeks to the soup and continue to simmer until leeks are tender for 3 to 5 minutes. Season the soup to taste with salt, pepper and nutmeg. Puree this mixture until smooth. When ready to serve, mix in sour cream or heavy cream. Garnish with chopped chives.

Makes 4 servings

This is an easy to make and heartwarming soup. An exquisite first course for a fun dinner! This soup can also be served cold.

A tradition
Be a Gentleman... Pour a Drink

Women do not pour their own drinks at the dinner table in Russia . Be a gentleman – always pour drinks for the women at your table!

Potato Soup with Cheese

4 Tbsp unsalted butter
1 large leek or 1 medium size onion
2 garlic cloves
4 cups chicken stock
4 large potatoes
1 large carrot
1 cup sour cream or heavy cream
1 cup grated sharp cheddar cheese
2 Tbsp dill
Salt and pepper

Melt butter in a skillet and cook the sliced leeks (or chopped onion) with minced garlic until tender. Bring chicken stock to a boil. Peel and cube potatoes and carrots. Lower the heat, add potatoes, carrots and simmer until the vegetables are tender. Add leeks to the soup and continue to simmer for 3 to 5 minutes. Puree this mixture until smooth. Add cheddar cheese and heavy cream or sour cream. Add dill. Season the soup to taste with salt and pepper. Garnish with chopped dill.

Makes 4 servings

Historically potatoes have been and continue to be one of the main staples of Russian cuisine. This soup is a classic delicious combination of potatoes, onion and dill. Sour cream, also a staple, is mixed in but can be served on the side. It goes well with potatoes and dill. Cheese adds richness to the soup and can be omitted if desired.

Beet Soup

4 cups chicken stock
4 Tbsp unsalted butter
1 medium size onion
2 garlic cloves
2 large potatoes
1 large carrot
1 celery stalk
2 large beets
1 celery root
½ cup heavy cream
2 Tbsp dill
Salt and pepper

Melt butter in a skillet and cook the chopped onion and minced garlic until tender. Peel and cube potatoes and carrots. Slice celery. Remove the outer layer of the celery root and cube. Bring chicken stock to a boil. Lower the heat, add vegetables and simmer until the vegetables are tender. Wash the beets and make a cut in each one. Cook beets covered in a microwavable dish until tender, 10-15 minutes. When ready, cool under cold water, peel, cut in large pieces and add to the soup. Puree this mixture until smooth. Add heavy cream to the desired consistency. Season the soup to taste with salt and pepper. Serve with sour cream and garnish with chopped dill.

Makes 4 servings

This soup looks stunning due to its deep and bright color and tastes absolutely delicious! Since it is pureed, it is a modern variation on a beet soup that has been served in Russia over the centuries. A tremendous dish to impress your guests!

Parsley & Tarragon Soup

4 cups chicken stock
3 Tbsp unsalted butter
1 cup chopped onion
1 large Russet potato
1 bunch fresh parsley
3 Tbsp tarragon
¼ cup half and half
Salt and pepper

Melt butter in a skillet over medium heat. Add onion and sauté for 5 minutes. Peel and cube the potato. Trim and chop parsley. Bring chicken stock to a boil. Lower the heat, add potatoes and cook for 10 minutes until tender. Add parsley and tarragon. Puree the mixture. Mix in half and half. Season with salt and pepper. Chill for 3 hours. When serving, sprinkle with parsley if desired.

Makes 4 servings

This is yet another variation on a potato soup, this time with parsley and tarragon. Fascinatingly, this combination makes a distinctive and delightful soup. It is designed to be served cold but it can be served warm as well.

A superstition
Do Not Give Knives as a Present

In Russia, a gift of knives is considered harmful to the friendship between a giver and a recipient.

Sorrel Soup

4 cups chicken stock
4 cups chopped sorrel
3 cups chopped spinach
2 Tbsp unsalted butter
1 medium size onion
1 stalk celery
2 medium size potatoes
¼ cup green onions
¼ cup heavy cream
2 hard boiled eggs
2 small cucumbers
Sour cream
Salt and pepper

Melt butter in a skillet over medium heat. Add chopped onion and celery and sauté for 5 minutes. Add green onions and sauté for another 5 minutes. Peel and cube the potato. Bring chicken stock to a boil. Lower the heat, add potatoes and cook for 10 minutes until tender. Add the onion and celery mixture and simmer until all vegetables are tender. Puree the mixture and return to heat. Add the sorrel and spinach and simmer until they wilt, for a minute or so. Turn off the heat and mix in heavy cream. Add salt and pepper. Chill. Serve each portion with one or two slices of egg, diced cucumbers and sour cream.

Makes 4 servings

Sorrel grows naturally in many regions of Russia and it is used in many dishes. It has distinctive leaves and a tart taste. I remember picking it when I was a child. In this recipe spinach is used as a filler. When sorrel is in season, definitely substitute spinach with additional sorrel. Heavy cream can be omitted especially if this soup is served on a hot summer day.

Lentil and Squash Soup

5 ½ cups chicken stock
1 lb butternut squash
1 cup lentils
1 cup chopped onion
1 bay leaf
1 medium carrot
1 celery stalk
1 small ripe tomato
¼ cup dry white wine
1 Tbsp curry powder
1 large garlic clove
2 Tbsp fresh lemon juice
Salt and pepper

Peel, seed and cube the squash. Cut all vegetables into small cubes. Combine the stock, squash, lentils, carrots, celery, onions and the bay leaf in a large saucepan. Simmer until lentils are tender, 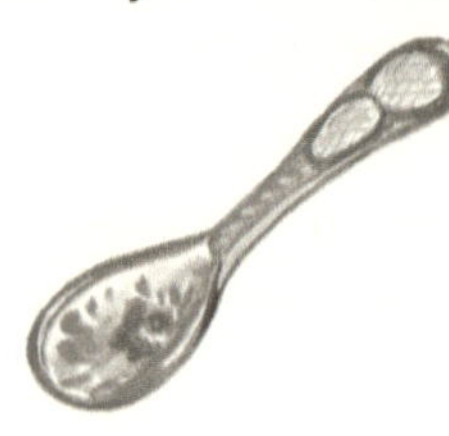 about 30 minutes, stirring occasionally. Add chopped tomato, white wine, curry powder and cook for additional 15 minutes. Thin soup if needed with additional broth. Add garlic pressed through the garlic press and puree the soup. Add lemon juice if desired and mix well. Sprinkle with parsley before serving. Add cayenne pepper if desired – this soup can be served spicy.

Makes 8 servings

This is a really savory soup! Great as a part of a Thanksgiving feast! It has a wonderful yellow orange color – a perfect fit!

Cream of Broccoli

4 cups chicken stock
2 lbs broccoli
1 large potato
4 Tbsp unsalted butter
1 large onion
2 garlic cloves
A dash of nutmeg
1 cup sour cream or heavy cream
Grated cheddar cheese

Peel and chop the onion. Melt butter in a skillet and cook the onions until translucent. Bring chicken stock to a boil. Separate broccoli florets from stems. Cut off the outer layer from stems and cut the remaining stems into bite size pieces. Peel and cube the potato. Bring chicken stock to a boil. Lower the heat, add potatoes and broccoli and simmer until potatoes are tender. Add onion to the soup and continue to simmer for 3 to 5 minutes. Remove from heat. Add garlic pressed through the garlic press. Mix in sour cream or heavy cream. Season the soup to taste with salt, pepper and nutmeg. Puree this mixture until smooth. Garnish with chopped chives and cheese if desired.

Makes 4 servings

Broccoli is not widely grown and used in Russia. Our family adopted this American recipe when we introduced new vegetable soups into our menu. We love this soup since it is easy to make and can be a filling but light lunch.

Shchi
(Classic Russian Cabbage Soup)

¾ lb any cut of beef with a bone
3 quarts water
1 medium size onion
2 medium size carrots
1 bay leaf
½ head green cabbage
2-3 potatoes
1 celery stalk
2 Tbsp each fresh parsley and dill
Salt

Peel and finely chop one onion, cube or shred one carrot and cook until tender in a skillet with olive oil. Put beef, a whole peeled onion, the carrot and the bay leaf in a large saucepan with water and bring to a boil. Skim the top, salt and cook on low heat until the meat is ready, approximately 40 minutes. Take out the meat and the veggies.

Peel and cut potatoes into small cubes, cube celery, thinly slice cabbage and add to the stock. Cook until done 10 minutes or so. Add the onion and carrot mixture to the soup and cook on low heat for 5 minutes or so. Add the cubed meat and bring to a boil. Remove from heat. Adjust seasoning and add parsley and dill. Serve with a dollop of sour cream.

Makes 8 servings

During the sixteenth and seventeenth centuries there were endless varieties of shchi made with meat, fish, barley, sorrel and so on. It was one of the main dishes served across Russia in both rich and poor families. Shchi was cooked in a large pot so that it lasted the family a couple of days. It is actually better the next day and even better the day after that because all the flavors blend. It goes well with rye or pumpernickel bread. And certainly with a shot of vodka. Enjoy!

Variations

You can experiment by adding many different vegetables to shchi. Below are a couple of variations that we enjoy:

- Add a chopped tomato and a tablespoon of tomato paste toward the end when adding the carrot mixture to the soup.
- Add garlic pressed through the garlic press together with herbs.
- Add cayenne pepper to taste.

A toast
Where are We Going?

A large powerful bird is flying in the sky. She is in command of the air current, her wings smoothly and gracefully cut through the air. There is a tiny bird flying nervously next to the large bird. She asks the large bird: "Where are we going, ah? Where?"

But the large bird maintains the silence, there is no answer. The little bird anxiously asks again: "Where are we flying? What's the destination? Ah?"

The large bird slowly turns its head to the little bird and says: "I have no idea…" Let's drink to us charting our own paths and knowing our destination!

Cream of Garlic Soup

¾ cup peeled garlic
3 Tbsp olive oil
2 ½ cups chicken stock
½ cup dry white wine
2 ½ cups milk
1 cup whipping cream
1 4 oz Russet potato
Salt and pepper

Blend garlic in the food processor to a coarse paste. Heat the oil in a heavy saucepan over low heat. Add garlic and cook for 10-12 minutes. Add stock and wine and bring to a boil. Reduce heat and simmer for 30 minutes. Add milk, cream and potato and simmer for 30 additional minutes. Puree the mixture. Season to taste with salt and pepper.

Makes 4 servings

Our family loves garlic as many Russians do. This soup is for garlic lovers. It is the best garlic soup that I have ever tasted – smooth and creamy!

A tradition
Have a Great Trip!

When guests are about to leave after a several day stay at a friends' house, it is a Russian custom for everyone in the party to sit down for a couple of minutes and quietly think about the impending journey, visualizing its success.

Rassolnik
(Classic Russian Soup with Pickles)

3 quarts water
1 ½ lb meat (beef or lamb) with a bone
2 Tbsp barley
2 medium size onions
1 carrot
5 half sour pickles
3 potatoes
3 bay leaves
Salt and pepper

Put barley into a small glass and cover with water. Rinse the meat and bring it to boil in water in a large saucepan. Skim the foam off the top. Add bay leaves and salt the stock. Cook for 45 minutes until the meat is tender. Remove the meat from the stock.

Finely chop onions and sauté in olive oil in a large skillet until translucent. Add diced carrots and cook for 5 minutes or so. Add the carrot mixture and the barley to the stock. Peel and cube potatoes and add to the stock. Cook until the potatoes are tender. Dice pickles and add to the stock, bring to a boil. Cut the meat into bite size pieces and add to the soup. Add parsley and adjust seasoning. Serve with sour cream, rye bread and butter.

Makes 8 servings

This is an unusual and delightful soup for a cold day. It has the sourness of pickles offset by the sweetness of onions, carrots and potatoes. It goes well with a shot of vodka!

Sweets

The sweet table in Russia is laid out when everyone is done with the main course. Sweet dishes are placed in the middle of the table so that guests can help themselves. This section includes classic Russian sweets that will provide a yummy conclusion to any meal.

Sweets

Kssel

4 cups water
1 cup cranberries
¾ cup sugar
2 Tbsp cornstarch

Dissolve cornstarch in 1 cup of cold water. Finely chop cranberries into a paste. Squeeze juices out of them and reserve in a jar in a refrigerator. Transfer the remaining peels into a saucepan with 3 cups of boiling water. Simmer for 10 minutes, cool, strain through a cheesecloth and squeeze out well. Add sugar to the remaining liquid, bring to a boil and slowly stir in the starch. Bring

to a boil again and turn off the heat. Stir in the reserved refrigerated cranberry juice. Cool and serve.

Makes 4 servings

This is a classic Russian sweet drink. If more starch is added, it can be served as dessert with whipped cream in individual cups. In our family we thicken it only slightly to make a distinctive drink that can be enjoyed on its own in the middle of the afternoon. Another popular berry in Russia that is used in this drink is black currants.

I remember when my daughter and I made this drink for a 'show and tell' for her class in middle school. We served this drink with Lemon Tarts (see separate recipe). Both delicacies were gone in the first five minutes! The children loved these unique, healthy and tasty Russian dishes!

A toast
Who Knows Whether It Is Good or Bad

There lived a wise man in a small village. All villagers went to him with their problems. One farmer came to the wise man and complained that his ox had died and it was the most terrible thing that had ever happened to him. The wise man responded: "Who knows whether it is good or bad."

Next week the farmer caught a horse that was roaming around his house. When he shared his joy with the wise man, his response was the same: "Who knows whether it is good or bad." Next day the farmer's son was thrown off the horse and broke his leg. The farmer lamented to the wise man: "This is really terrible, who will help me plow the fields?" The wise man listened and responded: "Who knows whether it is good or bad." The next day army recruiters arrived in the village to take every young man to war that had begun nearby. The farmer's son was spared because of his injury.

This story reminds us of the basic truth that we often ignore – that we really do not know what is going to happen to us in the future. Often we paint terrible scenarios in our minds about the future and we are wrong most of the time. Let's drink to keeping our cool regardless of what is happening to us since we can be reasonably certain that all will be well!

Limonnyi Pirog
(Lemon Tarts)

PASTRY
4 cups flour
Pinch of salt
1 tsp sugar
2 sticks cold unsalted butter
1 egg
1 Tbsp yeast
½ cup warm milk

FILLING
1 large whole lemon
1 ½ cups sugar
1 egg beaten for brushing

Combine flour, salt and sugar in a large mixing bowl. Cut cold butter into small pieces and add to the flour. Beat the egg slightly and add to the flour. Mix. Dissolve the yeast in the warm milk and add to the flour mixture in batches, mixing continually. Knead to a soft but not sticky pastry.

Cut lemon into small pieces discarding the seeds. Chop in the food processor with sugar.

Divide the pastry into two parts, one slightly larger than the other. Roll out the larger part, place on an oiled baking sheet and spread the lemon filling over it. Roll out the smaller pastry part and cover the pirog and pinch the sides tightly. Prick with a fork and brush the top with the beaten egg. Bake at 375° for 30 minutes or so. Cut into squares.

Makes 6 servings

This pirog can be served hot with whipped cream or cold as a wonderful snack. It is easy to make and is a delight to eat!

A tradition
Russian Royal Cuisine

Up to the 17th century the Russian Royal cuisine was not much different from the food served by ordinary people except for quantity. The Tsar's table was said to 'groan' under the load of food. A Royal dinner often included up to 200 dishes. The largest animals and fish were selected, so large as to be carried to the table by several people. The number of guests was also high. Ivan the Terrible (1500s) was reported to have invited 700 people to dinner!

Peter the Great (1672-1725) introduced European dishes into the Royal cuisine but it was really Catherine the Great (1729-1796) who adopted French cuisine and introduced a level of sophistication into the Royal cuisine. Dishes such as venison with truffles, quails, oysters, oranges, turtles, and exquisite desserts were adopted at that time.

Starting in the 18th century a Royal dinner consisted of 8 courses: a soup, such as shchi or uha, followed by zakuski, such as fish in aspic or pickled vegetables, followed by roast meat or poultry and then a boiled or baked fish course. Then came the pirogi, followed by kasha and then finally cakes, tarts and pastries. Ice cream, kisel or chocolate were served at the end. All these dishes were consumed in great quantity.

Under the rule of the last Tsar, Nicholas II, the Royal table became a blend of the native Russian dishes with a French touch.

Raspberry & Chocolate
Frozen Torte

CRUST
1 9 oz box chocolate graham crackers
1 stick unsalted butter

MOUSSE
½ cup crème de cassis
1 ½ tsp unflavored gelatin
2 12 oz packages of frozen raspberries
½ cup sugar
12 oz dark semisweet chocolate
2 cups whipping cream
1 Tbsp confectioners' sugar
1 tsp vanilla extract
1 box fresh raspberries

For crust: Finely chop cookie pieces in the food processor. Melt butter in a cup in a microwave or over low heat in a small saucepan. Blend into the cookie mixture until all crumbs are moist. Press mixture onto the bottom and halfway up the sides of a 9 inch diameter spring form pan. Freeze crust while preparing the mousse.

For mousse: Pour crème de cassis into a medium size saucepan, sprinkle the gelatin over the top and let stand for 20 minutes until the gelatin softens. Press thawed raspberries through a sieve into a large measuring cup and press tightly to squeeze out as much juice as you can. If you like raspberry seeds in the torte you can omit this step. Add 2 cups of raspberries or the same amount of the strained mixture to the gelatin. Add sugar. Stir over low heat until sugar and gelatin dissolve, about 3 minutes. Remove from heat and add the chocolate cut into small pieces and stir until melted. Cool but do not let it set.

Beat cream, confectioners' sugar and vanilla in a bowl to stiff peaks. Carefully, fold into the cool raspberry mixture in batches. Pour the mousse into the crust and smooth the top. Freeze until firm at least 4 hours. When ready to serve, release pan sides and decorate the top of the torte with fresh raspberries, whipped cream and shaved chocolate.

Makes 12 servings

This is a very festive presentation of a tremendously tasty combination of dark chocolate and raspberries! We usually make it for holiday parties. And it's convenient that this torte can be made a number of days ahead.

A toast
Making the Right Choice

An angel appeared in a young man's dream on Christmas Eve with the words: "I am generous today, oh, young one, I will fulfill one of your wishes. What would you like? Would you like such wealth that no one else on the planet has? Or wisdom that is incomparable with anything else? Or maybe such love that lights the stars and poets' hearts?"

The young man thought for awhile and decided on wisdom. The angel fulfilled the wish. Then asked: "And what would you say now, oh, the wisest of man?" And the wisest young man answered: "I should have taken money instead!"
...Let's drink to being able to always make the right choice!

Varenie
(Russian Preserves)

1 lb strawberries
½ cup sugar
1 tsp vanilla
Pinch cinnamon to taste

Rinse strawberries and cut off the leaves. Dry well with paper towels. Cut into small pieces and transfer into a small heavy saucepan. Add sugar and vanilla. Stir carefully. Put on very low heat for 10 minutes or so, stirring occasionally until all sugar dissolves. Cook on low heat for 15-30 minutes. The syrup will thicken. To test whether the jam is ready, take a small amount of the syrup and make a drop on your fingernail. If the syrup stays in the droplet, the jam is ready. If it runs off, turn the heat to medium or high to evaporate additional liquid. Store in jars in the refrigerator.

Makes 12 servings

The consistency of Russian jams is different from jams sold in the US, they have more liquid in them. You can add gelatin if desired to thicken.

Russians love to serve home cooked jams as a part of the afternoon tea. Jams are served alone or with bread and butter. Since Russians create any excuse to sit around the table to talk, indulging in tasting various jams is a great opportunity to do that. Usually the hostess serves three to four

various jams. Cranberry, black current and apple jams are the most popular. Russian cooks pride themselves on developing tasty fruit jam combinations. Now you can experiment with your own!

![B]anana Bread

1 cup mashed bananas
1 cup currants or raisins
½ cup dark rum
3 cups flour
Pinch of salt
1 tsp baking powder
1 tsp cinnamon
½ tsp nutmeg
½ cup unsalted butter
2 eggs
1 cup brown sugar
½ cup buttermilk

Pour rum into a glass, add currents and heat in a microwave for 1 minute until the rum is hot but not boiling. Let stand for at least an hour. Combine all dry ingredients in a mixing bowl. Set aside. Whip together softened butter, sugar and eggs. Stir buttermilk, banana and the currants mixture into the butter, sugar and eggs mix. Combine well. Add dry ingredients in batches, combining well until dry ingredients are moistened. Pour batter into a greased 9x5x3 inch pan. Bake at 350° for about an hour or until a tester, such as a toothpick, inserted in the middle comes out clean. Best if served warm with whipped cream.

Makes 1 loaf

Our family loves bananas. However, no one touches the overripe ones. We were throwing them away until we learned recently that we can freeze them. As a result, we always have plenty of bananas for this recipe at any time. Put them into a microwave for 10-20 seconds, peel and put the flesh into a cup – they are ready to be used!

Cranberry Molded Salad

CRANBERRY JAM
1 12 oz bag cranberries
1 cup sugar
1 apple
1 lemon

SALAD
1 ½ cup cranberry juice
2 ¼ oz packages unflavored gelatin

Pour cranberry juice into a small bowl, sprinkle with gelatin and let stand for 20 minutes until the gelatin softens.

Finely chop cranberries with sugar in a food processor. Transfer to a medium size saucepan. Put the pan over low heat until the sugar dissolves. Peel, core and dice the apple and add to the cranberry mixture. Add lemon zest. Cook for 8 minutes or so until cranberries are tender. Remove from heat. The jam can be stored in a jar in the refrigerator and enjoyed on its own. If making a salad, proceed with the rest of the recipe.

Stir in the gelatin mixture until the gelatin dissolves. Spoon the cranberry mixture into an 8 cup decorative mold. Cover and refrigerate until firm for at least 4 hours. When ready to serve unmold on a platter using hot towels.

Makes 8-10 servings

We make this festive and delicious salad for Thanksgiving. Goes superbly with turkey!

 Vatrushki
(Open Cheese Tartlets)

PASTRY
1 package puff pastry (2 sheets)
1 egg

FILLING
1 lb farmer's cheese
2 eggs
¼ cup sugar
1 Tbsp flour

For the filling: Slightly beat eggs with a fork in a bowl. Reserve a small amount for brushing in a separate container. Mix in the remaining filling ingredients.

Roll puff pastry out on a floured surface to ¼ inch thickness. Cut rounds 4 inch in diameter and put a tablespoon of the filling in each, folding the sides to make each vatrushka into a round shape. Pinch the sides well. Brush vatrushki with a slightly beaten egg. Place vatrushki on a greased baking sheet, cover with a towel and let stand for 20 minutes. Bake at 350° for 25-30 minutes.

Makes 15 vatrushki

Russians love to serve sweet pastry with tea. This is the Russian equivalent of cheese-filled Danish pastries. There are as many variations of these mouthwatering sweets as there are cooks. This version is easy to make and absolutely scrumptious!

Russian Apple Pie

PASTRY
1 package puff pastry (2 sheets)
1 egg

FILLING
3 Granny Smith apples
6 oz raisins or 2 Tbsp sugar
1 Tbsp cinnamon (optional)

Roll both pieces of puff pastry out on a floured surface to ¼ inch thickness. Transfer one piece to a greased baking sheet. Core, peel and quarter apples. Cut into thin slices crosswise. Put cut apples on the pastry on the baking sheet. Evenly add raisins. If you prefer the pie without raisins, sprinkle sugar on the apples instead. Cover the apple layer with another piece of puff pastry and pinch the sides well to close. Punch holes in the top pastry with a fork. Brush with slightly beaten egg. Cook for 30 minutes at 350°. Cut into slices and serve.

Makes 6 servings

This pie is distinctly different from its counterparts in the US. There is no starch in the filling. This version uses the prepared puff pastry. My mother makes the dough from scratch (see Poppy Seed Roll for the recipe). She makes the pie open, just slightly pinching the dough on the sides and decorating with thin strips of dough crisscrossing the top of the apples layer. Both versions are out of this world!

Chocolate Mousse

8 oz semi-sweet dark chocolate
½ cup water
5 eggs
3 Tbsp rum
½ cup heavy cream
1 Tbsp confectioners' sugar
½ tsp vanilla extract

Prepare 6-8 serving cups. Cut the chocolate into small pieces and put them into a small heavy saucepan with water over very low heat. Stir continuously until the chocolate dissolves. Stir in the rum. Let cool for 5-10 minutes. In the meantime separate the egg yolks from whites. Beat the egg yolks one at a time into the warm chocolate mixture. In a large mixing bowl beat the egg whites to soft peaks. Add the chocolate mixture to the egg whites in batches, folding it carefully into the egg whites until well blended. The mixture will be smooth and shiny. Pour the mousse in the serving cups and put into the refrigerator to set.

Whip the heavy cream with confectioners' sugar and the vanilla extract to soft peaks. When the mousse is set, add a dollop of whipped cream to each cup. Garnish with fresh raspberries and thin slices of almonds if desired.

Makes 6-8 servings

This is one of the easiest desserts to make and it's extremely popular with guests because it is simply irresistible!

Poppy Seed Roll

DOUGH (as my Mom makes it)
2 cups milk
1 stick unsalted butter
1 ¼ oz package dry yeast
1 tsp sugar
3 cups flour
Pinch of salt

FILLING
2 cups poppy seeds
½ cup milk
½ cup sugar
3 Tbsp honey
2 eggs
2 Tbsp unsalted butter

For the dough: heat milk until warm, dissolve butter in it, sprinkle yeast on top, and add salt and sugar. Mix well. Gradually add flour, mixing with your hands. The dough should come off your hands easily when it is ready. Cover with a towel and let stand for an hour and a half.

For the filling: Heat the milk in a small saucepan until hot. Pour poppy seeds into the milk and let stand for 5 minutes. Using a slotted spoon transfer the poppy seeds into the food processor and add one tablespoon of milk. Grind the seeds into a paste. If necessary add more milk. Transfer into a mixing bowl and combine with sugar, honey, eggs and melted butter. Mix well.

On a floured surface roll the dough into a 12 inch square ¼ inch thick. Spread the filling on the dough and roll it tightly into a roll. Cover with a towel and let stand for 20 minutes. Place the roll on a greased baking sheet, brush with a slightly beaten egg and bake at 350° for 45 minutes. Cut into slices when cooled.

Makes 8 servings

This is one of the most popular desserts in the western part of the former USSR, especially in Estonia and Latvia. Great with tea or coffee. Enjoy it while it lasts. It usually disappears really quickly.

A tradition
Banya (Russian Sauna)

Russia is known for its cold weather. One of the winter traditions is a visit to a banya.

In the countryside banya is a tiny wooden building consisting of a small front room where clothing is left and a sauna-like room with a stove. In contrast to a sauna, banya has wet steam and you do not just sit there and enjoy the heat. You receive a 'massage' – a whipping of your body with birch branches, if you happen to have an expert in your party who can do this. Performing this procedure is an art. In many cases, the branches do not touch your body per say but just intensify the hot air pressure on the skin. This process induces deep relaxation and tremendous blood circulation. After a visit to a banya Russians say that they feel as if they have been reborn.

It is customary to jump into a lake, roll in the snow or dive into a cold pool during breaks from the heat. Then you fortify yourself with food and drink, most often vodka and zakuski, and then repeat!

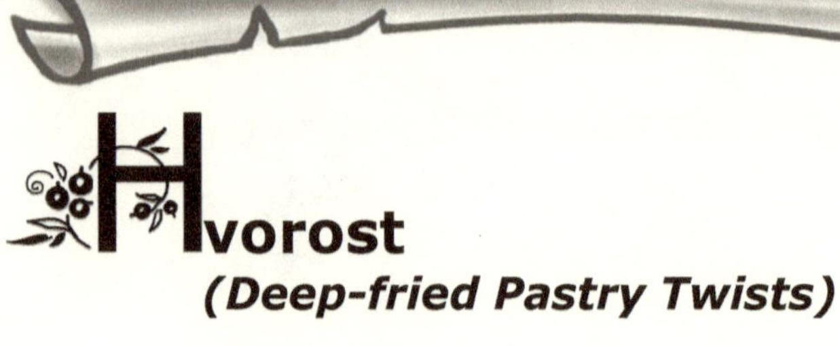

Hvorost
(Deep-fried Pastry Twists)

1 egg
1 Tbsp sugar
3 Tbsp sour cream
1 Tbsp vodka
1 cup flour maximum
Vegetable oil for frying

Combine the first 4 ingredients and gradually add flour until the dough is soft and smooth. Some flour might be left over.

Roll the dough on a floured surface ¼ inch thick. Cut strips of dough 1 inch wide and 4 inches long. Make an incision in the middle of the strip leaving about ½ inch uncut on both sides and pull one end of the strip through the incision. This will make the pastry into a twist.

In a medium size saucepan that can hold the twists lengthwise heat the vegetable oil. There should be about an inch of oil in the bottom of the pan. Slowly immerse the twists into the oil using a slotted spoon. Cook until golden brown. Transfer to a plate and sprinkle with confectioners' sugar.

Makes 6-8 servings

Simply irresistible!

Sharlotka
("Guest-at-the-Doorstep" Russian Apple Charlotte)

4 large apples
3 eggs
½ cup sugar
1 cup flour
1 tsp vanilla extract (optional)

Butter a 9 inch spring form pan. Core, peel, quarter and slice apples crosswise into ¼ inch slices. Place into the pan. In a large bowl beat the eggs with sugar with a mixer. Mix in the vanilla extract. The mixture will be light yellow and will form ribbons when the beaters are lifted out of the bowl. Gradually mix in flour in batches. The batter will be rather thick. Pour the batter over the apples. The batter and the apples should be even. If not, add apples. Bake at 350° for 45 minutes until the top is golden and a tester, such as a toothpick, inserted in the middle comes out clean. Serve with whipped cream or ice cream.

Makes 6 servings

In the times of the Soviet Union telephones were rare and it was customary for guests to just stop by without notice. This dish could be prepared quickly since most of the ingredients were almost always on hand. It is a delectable concoction! You will undoubtedly be asked for the recipe when you serve it.

A toast
Let's Have a Drink!

Georgians sit around a huge table drinking and eating. The tamada gets up:

- Gogi, say a toast!

- Let's have a drink!

- Great, Gogi! Well said!

A couple minutes later the tamada gets up again:

- Gogi, say a toast!

- Let's have a drink!

- Wonderful, Gogi!

In a couple of minutes, the tamada gets up again:

- Vano, say a toast!

- We are gathered around this tremendous table so that…

- No, no, my dear, not this way… Gogi, say a toast!

- Let's have a drink!

So… let's just have a drink!